The **Essential** Buyer's Guide

TRIUMPH

TR4/4A & TR5/250

All models 1961 to 1968

Your marque experts:
Andy Child and Sarah Battyll

T0373727

VELOCE PUBLISHING
THE PUBLISHER OF FINE AUTOMOTIVE BOOKS

Essential Buyer's Guide Series

Alfa Romeo Alfasud (Metcalfe)
Alfa Romeo Alfetta: all saloon/sedan models 1972 to 1984 & coupé models 1974 to 1987 (Metcalfe)
Alfa Romeo Giulia GT Coupé (Booker)
Alfa Romeo Giulia Spider (Booker)
Audi TT (Davies)
Audi TT Mk2 2006 to 2014 (Durnan)
Austin-Healey Big Healeys (Trummel)
BMW Boxer Twins (Henshaw)
BMW E30 3 Series 1981 to 1994 (Hosier)
BMW GS (Henshaw)
BMW X5 (Saunders)
BMW Z3 Roadster (Fishwick)
BMW Z4: E85 Roadster and E86 Coupé including M and Alpina 2003 to 2009 (Smitheram)
BSA 350, 441 & 500 Singles (Henshaw)
BSA 500 & 650 Twins (Henshaw)
BSA Bantam (Henshaw)
Citroën 2CV (Paxton)
Citroën ID & DS (Heilig)
Cobra Replicas (Ayre)
Corvette C2 Sting Ray 1963-1967 (Falconer)
Datsun 240Z 1969 to 1973 (Newlyn)
DeLorean DMC-12 1981 to 1983 (Williams)
Ducati Bevel Twins (Falloon)
Ducati Desmodue Twins (Falloon)
Ducati Desmoquattro Twins – 851, 888, 916, 996, 998, ST4 1988 to 2004 (Falloon)
Fiat 500 & 600 (Bobbitt)
Ford Capri (Paxton)
Ford Escort Mk1 & Mk2 (Williamson)
Ford Model A – All Models 1927 to 1931 (Buckley)
Ford Model T – All models 1909 to 1927 (Barker)
Ford Mustang – First Generation 1964 to 1973 (Cook)
Ford Mustang (Cook)
Ford RS Cosworth Sierra & Escort (Williamson)
Harley-Davidson Big Twins (Henshaw)
Hillman Imp (Morgan)
Hinckley Triumph triples & fours 750, 900, 955, 1000, 1050, 1200 – 1991-2009 (Henshaw)
Honda CBR FireBlade (Henshaw)
Honda CBR600 Hurricane (Henshaw)
Honda SOHC Fours 1969-1984 (Henshaw)
Jaguar E-Type 3.8 & 4.2 litre (Crespin)
Jaguar E-type V12 5.3 litre (Crespin)
Jaguar Mark 1 & 2 (All models including Daimler 2.5-litre V8) 1955 to 1969 (Thorley)
Jaguar New XK 2005-2014 (Thorley)
Jaguar S-Type – 1999 to 2007 (Thorley)
Jaguar X-Type – 2001 to 2009 (Thorley)
Jaguar XJ-S (Crespin)
Jaguar XJ6, XJ8 & XJR (Thorley)
Jaguar XK 120, 140 & 150 (Thorley)
Jaguar XK8 & XKR (1996-2005) (Thorley)
Jaguar/Daimler XJ 1994-2003 (Crespin)
Jaguar/Daimler XJ40 (Crespin)
Jaguar/Daimler XJ6, XJ12 & Sovereign (Crespin)
Kawasaki Z1 & Z900 (Orritt)
Land Rover Discovery Series 1 (1989-1998) (Taylor)
Land Rover Discovery Series II (1998-2004) (Taylor)

Land Rover Series I, II & IIA (Thurman)
Land Rover Series III (Thurman)
Lotus Seven replicas & Caterham 7: 1973-2013 (Hawkins)
Mazda MX-5 Miata (Mk1 1989-97 & Mk2 98-2001) (Crook)
Mazda RX-8 (Parish)
Mercedes Benz Pagoda 230SL, 250SL & 280SL roadsters & coupés (Bass)
Mercedes-Benz 190: all 190 models (W201 series) 1982 to 1993 (Parish)
Mercedes-Benz 280-560SL & SLC (Bass)
Mercedes-Benz SL R129-series 1989 to 2001 (Parish)
Mercedes-Benz SLK (Bass)
Mercedes-Benz W123 (Parish)
Mercedes-Benz W124 – All models 1984-1997 (Zoporowski)
MG Midget & A-H Sprite (Horler)
MG TD, TF & TF1500 (Jones)
MGA 1955-1962 (Crosier)
MGB & MGB GT (Williams)
MGF & MG TF (Hawkins)
Mini (Paxton)
Morris Minor & 1000 (Newell)
Moto Guzzi 2-valve big twins (Falloon)
New Mini (Collins)
Norton Commando (Henshaw)
Peugeot 205 GTI (Blackburn)
Piaggio Scooters – all modern two-stroke & four-stroke automatic models 1991 to 2016 (Willis)
Porsche 911 (964) (Streather)
Porsche 911 (993) (Streather)
Porsche 911 (996) (Streather)
Porsche 911 (997) – Model years 2004 to 2009 (Streather)
Porsche 911 (997) – Second generation models 2009 to 2012 (Streather)
Porsche 911 Carrera 3.2 (Streather)
Porsche 911SC (Streather)
Porsche 924 – All models 1976 to 1988 (Hodgkins)
Porsche 928 (Hemmings)
Porsche 930 Turbo & 911 (930) Turbo (Streather)
Porsche 944 (Higgins)
Porsche 981 Boxster & Cayman (Streather)
Porsche 986 Boxster (Streather)
Porsche 987 Boxster and Cayman 1st generation (2005-2009) (Streather)
Porsche 987 Boxster and Cayman 2nd generation (2009-2012) (Streather)
Range Rover – First Generation models 1970 to 1996 (Taylor)
Rolls-Royce Silver Shadow & Bentley T-Series (Bobbitt)
Royal Enfield Bullet (Henshaw)
Subaru Impreza (Hobbs)
Sunbeam Alpine (Barker)
Triumph 350 & 500 Twins (Henshaw)
Triumph Bonneville (Henshaw)
Triumph Stag (Mort)
Triumph Thunderbird, Trophy & Tiger (Henshaw)
Triumph TR4/4A & TR5/250 - All models 1961 to 1968 (Child and Battyl)
Triumph TR6 (Williams)
Triumph TR7 & TR8 (Williams)
Velocette 350 & 500 Singles 1946 to 1970 (Henshaw)
Vespa Scooters – Classic 2-stroke models 1960-2008 (Paxton)
Volkswagen Bus (Copping)
Volvo 700/900 Series (Beavis)
Volvo P1800/1800S, E & ES 1961 to 1973 (Murray)
VW Beetle (Copping)
VW Golf GTI (Copping)

www.veloce.co.uk

First published in October 2018 by Veloce Publishing Limited, Veloce House, Parkway Farm Business Park, Middle Farm Way, Poundbury, Dorchester, DT1 3AR, England. Tel +44 (0)1305 260068 / Fax 01305 250479 / e-mail info@veloce.co.uk / web www.veloce.co.uk or www.velocebooks.com.
ISBN: 978-1-787112-85-8 UPC: 6-6-36847-01285-4.

Introduction
– the purpose of this book

Welcome! If you're reading this, we guess you might already own a TR, but, more likely, you're seriously considering buying one. So, why choose one of these cars when there are lots of classic sports cars to pick from? In our view, the reason is simple – they are some of the very best examples from the golden era of classic British sports cars, the 1960s!

The TR4 has a centrally-placed 'TR4' bonnet badge. Its sidelights are in the grille, not on the wings.

Triumph's TR range of sports cars shows a clear evolution of an outstanding original design. In simple terms, it went as follows:

1961 TR4 Essentially a TR3a rolling chassis and a much improved (and handsome) body, with wind-up windows courtesy of Michelotti of Italy. It saved Triumph from financial ruin!

1965 TR4A A TR4 with new independent rear suspension (IRS), and a revised chassis to accommodate it.

1967 TR5 A TR4a with Triumph's newer six-cylinder 2500cc engine and Lucas petrol injection (PI), which replaced the older four-cylinder carburettor-based unit.

1967 TR250 A detuned TR5 with carburettors, instead of the PI system. It was made in left-hand drive (LHD) for the 'important' American market.

1968 TR6 The TR5's and TR250's front and rear were restyled to produce the TR6; available with either PI or carburettors.

Within the TR4/4A/5/250 range, there are two other less well-known variants that we ought to mention, as you might occasionally find them for sale and wonder what they are!

The TR4A has a centrally-placed circular 'Triumph World' bonnet badge. Its sidelights are on the wings, not in the grille.

The TR5 has an offset 'TR5' bonnet badge. Its sidelights are on the wings.

The TR250 has an offset 'TR250' bonnet badge. Its sidelights are on the wings, and it normally has a transverse bonnet decal (which may not be present on the car you're looking at).

Live Axle (Non-IRS) TR4A Produced at the request of the American market for cost reasons. It used the solid TR4 rear axle with the TR4a chassis. When new, the car's rear handling and roadholding were poor; today's modern tyres have significantly improved this. Identified by the lack of an 'IRS' badge and by semi-elliptic cart springs at the rear, they were all originally LHD.

Dove GTR4 and GTR4A The fastback 2+2 was a conversion made by Triumph dealers, Dove of Wimbledon, who added a steel roof, rear seats, and a tailgate to the standard TR4/4a. The new roof added weight to an otherwise clever bit of packaging. Most purchasers of these like the rarity value compared to an MGB GT or Triumph GT6.

Thanks

We are indebted to various members of the TR Register who provided some of the pictures.

The GTR Dove conversion features a fastback coupé-style roof and tailgate. The position of the sidelights shows that this Dove is based on a TR4A IRS.

Contents

The Essential Buyer's Guide™ currency
At the time of publication a BG unit of currency "●" equals approximately £1.00/US$1.33/Euro 1.13. Please adjust to suit current exchange rates using Sterling as the base currency.

1 Is it the right car for you?
– marriage guidance

TRs are excellent 1960s sports cars with good performance. They're best on traffic-free country roads, but are also fine on motorways, especially if overdrive is fitted. They don't like hot traffic jams – just like most TR drivers!

Featuring a non-standard steering wheel, this TR4 has a painted metal dashboard and black central console, which contains four minor instruments.

The TR4A/5/250 has a wooden dashboard. This TR4A has an original-style teak dashboard.

This TR5 has an upgraded Burr Walnut dashboard. It has a non-standard steering wheel. A smaller sports wheel is often fitted.

Tall and short drivers
This is a good sized sports car that is comfortable for almost everybody – it's certainly not a tight fit like a Spitfire. The maximum seatback to pedal distance is 1.01m/3ft. Maximum headroom above the seat cushion is about 0.86m/2ft 10in.

Weight of controls
Steering is not power assisted, but is reasonably light (unless a very small steering wheel is fitted), and very direct. The brake and clutch pedals are heavier than most modern cars, though perfectly acceptable. The gear change is fairly heavy, yet satisfyingly direct none-the-less.

Will it fit the garage?
Length: 3.937m/12ft 11in. Width: 1.470m/4ft 10in.

Interior space
The cabin is spacious at 1.232m/4ft 0.5in between doors. If a soft top is fitted, it will occupy the rear occasional seats when down (except TR4). The optional surrey top, with removable canvas section, leaves the rear shelf empty.

Luggage capacity
The boot is small at $0.16m^3/5.6ft^3$. However, it has ample room for a picnic hamper or overnight bags, with more room behind the seats (unless the soft top is folded down).

Running costs
These cars are relatively economical to run, especially when compared to the Jaguar E-type or Mercedes Pagoda. The usual service interval is 6000 miles (10,000km), or every 12 months.

Usability
Many owners don't use their TR4/4A/5/250s on a daily basis, but often drive a modern car in the winter when the roads are salted.

Parts availability and costs
Parts availability is excellent. See chapter 16 for a list of suppliers in Europe and the USA. See chapter 2 for costs.

Classic car insurance
It pays to shop around to get the best deal (which might not be the cheapest). Always go for an agreed value comprehensive policy, and don't undervalue your car.

Investment potential
TR4/4A/5/250s don't depreciate, so they represent the best of both worlds – excellent investments that are great to drive. Values partly depend on how carefully the car's been looked after. Care for your TR, and it'll repay you handsomely.

The boot area is quite large for a sports car. The floorboard that covers the spare wheel, and the trimboards covering the fuel tank and sides, are not yet fitted to this car.

Foibles
- The PI system on the TR5 had a reputation for unreliability. This simply isn't true now, as most cars use a Bosch fuel pump instead of the troublesome Lucas unit.
- Modern unleaded fuels necessitate a head conversion or the use of a fuel additive.
- The TR4A/5/250 independent rear suspension squats noticeably under acceleration. A telescopic rear shock absorber conversion cures this.
- Chassis weaknesses on the TR4A/5/250s exist around the front suspension and rear differential brackets. Extra strengthening brackets cure this – most cars will already have them.

Only the TR4 has a soft top that's stored in the boot. The rear seat area is available for luggage or small passengers when the roof is down.

- A weak crankshaft thrust washer design means you must not sit in traffic jams with your foot on the clutch pedal. Select neutral and release the pedal whenever stationary to avoid trouble.
- Warm a cold engine before driving enthusiastically to avoid unnecessary wear and blue oil smoke from the exhaust. Treat the engine sympathetically, and it will repay you.

Plus points
Chrome 'n' fins classic look, enthusiastic engines, carefree top-down stylish motoring.

Minus points
It'll have its off days and break occasionally. Rust issues need to be dealt with promptly.

British sports car alternatives
Austin-Healey 100/4 and 3000, MGA/B/C, Sunbeam Alpine, Morgan Plus 4, and Triumph TR6.

2 Cost considerations
– affordable, or a money pit?

Purchase
The low initial cost of a rusty project car can look tempting, but beware! They are almost always more expensive to restore than the price of a good one. So, buy the best you can afford, but be aware that the most expensive one may not be the best. Use this book to accurately assess the true condition of any TR for sale.

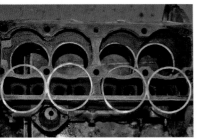

The TR4/4A four-cylinder engine has wet liners that rest on these two figure-of-eight seals. On worn out engines, these seals corrode and leak coolant water into the sump.

Servicing
A classic car needs more servicing than its modern counterpart. When new, the TR had a service interval of 6000 miles; today most owners do an annual service.

The annual government safety check (where applicable) ensures your TR is safe and is a useful way of proving to insurers that your car was roadworthy in the event of an accident.

Spare parts
Almost all the parts that you could need are readily available. Chapter 16 lists the main suppliers. Don't forget to search the Internet too.

The following tables are a guide to current prices (excluding VAT and other taxes):

New mechanical parts	TR4/4A	TR5/250
Exhaust (excluding manifold)	x300	x330
Stainless manifold and exhaust	x200	x250
Radiator (exchange)	x275/x238	x182
Set reinforced hoses	x24	x28
Alternator or dynamo (Xch)	x50 (dynamo)	x53 (alternator)
Distributor (exchange)	x146	x158
Front shock absorbers (each)	x15	x15
Brake servo	(Not fitted)	x102
Brake master cylinder	x50	x50
Front brake discs (each)	x30	x30
Front brake pads (Kevlar)	x45	x45
Rear brake shoes (set)	x20	x20
Rear slave cylinder (each)	x15	x15
Clutch set	x100	x95
Clutch master cylinder	x34	x30
Clutch slave cylinder	x25	x25
Gearbox rebuild	x300	x300
Overdrive rebuild	x300	x300
Cylinder head gasket set	x25	x25
Unleaded cylinder head (exchange)	x320	x335
Differential rebuild	x320	x320

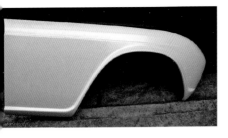

Genuine original Stanpart wings (and other panels) are rare, and thus can be quite expensive.

Rear hubs (exchange)	(Not fitted)	x100
Starter motor (HiTorq)	x175	x175
Bosch PI fuel pump kit	(Not fitted)	x265
Rebuilt PI unit (exchange)	(Not fitted)	x245
PI injectors (each, exchange)	(Not fitted)	x24
Carburettor fuel pump	x20	x20

Body parts

Front/rear wings (each)	x602	x602
Door	x430	x430
Door skin	x183	x183
Boot lid	x720	x720
Windscreen	x65	x65
Interior trim panel set (vinyl)	x295	x295
Wool carpet set	x262	x262
Seat cover kit (vinyl)	x330	x330
New leather-covered seats	x645	x645
Wooden dashboard/Fascia	(Not fitted)	x272
New soft top cover (vinyl)	x278	x278
New soft top cover (mohair)	x446	x446
New rear light clusters (pair)	x200	x200

If the clutch starts to slip, it's important that each of its three components are replaced: the pressure plate (cover), friction (clutch) plate, and release bearing.

The six-cylinder TR5/250 engine doesn't have wet liners. This TR5 PI unit has six black injector pipes over the engine rocker cover (arrow a), and the injection metering unit underneath the distributor (arrow b).

3 Living with a TR
– will you get along together?

If you're new to classic car ownership and wonder what it's like, consider this illustration. The highest mountain in Wales is Mount Snowdon. For most people, there are two popular routes to the summit:

- The narrow gauge railway transports you up effortlessly, but in isolation from the mountain.
- The southern footpath takes you via the Gladstone Rock, a river, waterfalls and much beautiful scenery. You really see, smell, feel, hear, and experience the mountain.

Similarly, a modern car, like the train, will effortlessly get you from A to B in an insulated cocoon. A classic car, like the footpath, is altogether more involving. What you get is a satisfying driving experience, a sense of achievement, and a smile on your face!

So, what's the reality of living with a TR4/4A/5/250?

Engine

TR4/4A The four-cylinder 2138cc engine is coarser than the TR5/250 engine. It doesn't really like revving, but will pull from very low revs with enthusiasm, so gear changes are infrequent. Fuel consumption is typically 25-35mpg. It burns a little oil, consuming a pint every 600 miles on average, so check the level before each journey. The 0-60mph acceleration time is around 11s, faster than an MGB or Alpine.

TR5/250 The six-cylinder 2498cc engine is smoothly free-revving with good mid-range torque. The 150bhp fuel-injected TR5 has a 0-60mph time of 8.8s, while the 111bhp detuned carburetted TR250 has a 0-60mph time of 10.6s. Fuel economy is typically 20-30mpg.

General Expect the engines to drip a little oil. They all have a manual choke control to use when starting from cold. Pull it out fully and rotate ¼ turn clockwise to lock it out before starting the engine, then, progressively ease it back in as the engine warms. Do this too soon, and the engine will hesitate. Leave it out too long, and the engine will stall at tickover whilst using too much fuel.

A TR4/4A engine bay is spacious and easy to work in. This car has a thin fanbelt conversion and an alternator in place of the original dynamo.

The TR5/250 engine bay is slightly less spacious than that of the TR4/4A. This TR5 PI engine has a non-standard K&N air filter for enhanced performance.

TR4/4A dashboard: 1 air vent; 2 glovebox;
3 temperature gauge; 4 oil pressure gauge; 5 tonneau
retainer; 6 fuel gauge; 7 ammeter gauge; 8 ashtray;
9 Panel lights dimmer; 10 windscreen washers;
11 windscreen wipers; 12 ignition switch; 13 choke;
14 heater vents control; 15 fan blower switch; 16 light
switch stalk; 17 speedometer; 18 ignition light;
19 indicators light; 20 tachometer; 21 overdrive switch
stalk; 22 indicator switch stalk.

TR5/250 dashboard: 1 bullseye air
vent; 2 glovebox; 3 temperature gauge; 4 oil pressure
gauge; 5 fuel gauge; 6 ammeter gauge; 7 panel
lights dimmer; 8 tonneau retainer; 9 heater vents
control; 10 fan; 11 heater temperature; 12 ignition
switch; 13 choke; 14 tachometer; 15 speedometer;
16 windscreen wipers; 17 light switch stalk;
18 windscreen washers; 19 indicator switch stalk;
20 overdrive switch stalk.

Clutch pedal

It's fairly heavy and must be pushed fully to the floor to disengage. Remember the crankshaft thrust washer is weak, so do not sit in traffic jams with the clutch pedal depressed. Instead, knock the gearlever into neutral, take your foot off the pedal, and all will be well with the engine.

Gearbox

The gearchange is heavy but satisfyingly positive. A desirable option is an overdrive, which effectively gives the car a fifth gear, and is operated via a steering column switch. Only engage or disengage it when not accelerating or decelerating to avoid snatching the transmission (some drivers briefly disengage the clutch). Overdrive fifth gives you effortless cruising on motorways. Interestingly, overdrive also works on second and third gears, so you actually have a seven-speed gearbox!

Brakes

These are always discs on the front and drums on the rear, with servo assistance on the TR5/250. The handbrake on the TR4A/5/250 is normal, but on the TR4 it's 'fly off' in operation. Engage it by pulling it on and pushing the button in. Release it by pulling it on further until the button pops up (flies off), then release the lever. When parking safely on a hill, always select first gear, as well as the handbrake.

Handling and roadholding

Handling and roadholding are very good, especially with modern radial tyres. The TR4 had a reputation for being tail-happy, but modern tyres cure this. The TR4A/5/250 has soft rear shock absorbers that allow squat under acceleration.

A telescopic shock absorber conversion kit rectifies this, and most cars already have this fitted.

Seats
These are generally comfortable, although some owners fit aftermarket Mazda MX5 seats for extra support. Often the original seat foam collapses, and you end up sitting almost on the floor. New seat foam cures this.

Soft top
TR4 The roof fully detaches from the car for storage in the boot. It's fiddly to erect, but allows the use of occasional rear seats with the soft top down.
TR4A/5/250 It has a fixed back rail and folds down onto the occasional rear seats. It's worth learning how to fold it properly, so you don't crease the plastic windows. Search the internet for instructional videos. Be very careful when erecting or folding the soft top on a cold day as the windows can crack.
General To keep it in good condition, always raise it when the car is unused.

The desirable Surrey Top option should come with both a steel roof panel (arrowed) and a vinyl soft top (fitted to the car). The steel roof is too big to fit in the boot.

Surrey top
Be aware that the steel roof won't fit in the boot.

Fuel
All of the engines prefer premium grade fuel to avoid pinking (pre-ignition) under acceleration. Always have the fuel tank at least a quarter full, especially with the TR5 PI, where fuel starvation, especially round left corners, causes an immediate power loss. Modern fuel likes a cool engine bay, so consider fitting an extra electric cooling fan.

Punctures
Jack Buy yourself a scissor jack for roadside punctures. The official jack goes through two large holes in the floors and is useless! Always jack on the suspension or chassis – never the sills or bodywork.
Wire wheels The right-hand side wheel spinners have left-hand threads – all spinners have the word 'undo' and an direction arrow. Always use the hide end of a copper-hide mallet to avoid bruising the chrome finish; never use a hammer.

Security
There isn't a steering lock, and it's no use locking the doors when there's a soft top to undo or slash. Adding a hidden ignition immobilising switch (and a PI pump switch on the TR5) and a mechanical steering wheel lock are popular theft deterrents. For the best security, fit a good alarm system and/or a vehicle tracker.

4 Relative values
– which model for you?

Many factors affect the price of a classic car, so it's impossible to give any absolute figures. However, the following tables provide guidance on the values of the TR4, TR4A, TR5, and TR250. These figures are also affected by the desirable and undesirable features listed in chapter 12. The best guide to price comes from TRs actually on sale now in various classic car magazine and online. These sources also publish useful price guide listings.

A genuine TR5 with all the desirable options is the most expensive model, so all others are valued relative to that:

Model	Value relative to an unconverted O/D TR5
TR4 unconverted (steering wheel on wrong side) with O/D	50%
TR4 unconverted (s/wheel on wrong side) without O/D	45%
TR4 LHD/RHD conversion with O/D	45%
TR4 without O/D and LHD/RHD conversion	40%
TR4A unconverted with O/D	55%
TR4A unconverted without O/D	50%
TR4A LHD/RHD conversion with O/D	50%
TR4A without O/D and LHD/RHD conversion	45%
TR4A live axle (non-IRS)	35%
TR5 unconverted with O/D	100%
TR5 unconverted without O/D	90%
TR5 LHD/RHD conversion with O/D	90%
TR5 without O/D and LHD/RHD conversion	80%
TR250 unconverted with O/D	70%
TR250 unconverted without O/D	65%
TR250 RHD conversion	65%
TR250 without O/D and RHD conversion	60%
(N.B. All TR250s were LHD)	

If you fancy a TR5, but can't stretch your budget that far, an early (pre-1973) TR6 is mechanically identical. However, it isn't nearly as handsome!

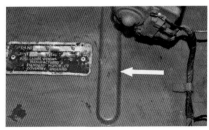

Underneath the wiper motor in the engine bay, the swage pressing in the panel indicates that it is likely original.

The majority of TR4As were made with Independent Rear Suspension (IRS), and have an extra badge on the boot lid.

This is a TR4A IRS chassis, viewed from the front. Note the main outer chassis rails are truncated just ahead of the rear suspension, and join to the trailing arm limbs.

The TR5's high-pressure Lucas fuel pump is often exchanged for a Bosch unit. Optionally, the Bosch pump can be fitted outside the boot to aid cooling, and reduces fumes.

This is non-IRS TR4A chassis. The rear spring crossmember has been removed to give room for the axle. It was sold in the US only.

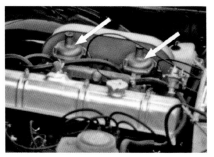

This TR250 engine has twin Stromberg carburettors (arrowed). The distributor sits lower because there is no metering unit drive assembly.

The PI metering unit on this TR5 engine is located below the distributor. The injector's six fuel pipes pass over the engine to the unit (arrowed). This car has had non-standard auxiliary fuse boxes fitted beside the wiper motor.

Yes, we know, it's a TR6! An early TR6 (PI or carburettors) has identical performance to a TR5/250, but is cheaper to buy. Of course It's not nearly as handsome as a TR5/250, but, if your budget is tight, it might be worth considering.

5 Before you view
– be well informed

To avoid the frustration of a car not matching your expectations, remember to ask specific questions when you call before viewing. Excitement can make even the most obvious things slip your mind, and, asking specific questions makes it harder for sellers to answer dishonestly. Try to assess the seller's attitude and demeanour, and decide how comfortable you are buying a car from them.

Where is the car?
Work out the cost of travelling to view a car. For a rare model, or the exact specification you want, it may be worth travelling, but, if the vehicle is common, decide first how far you're prepared to go. Viewing locally advertised cars can add to your knowledge for very little effort, so don't dismiss them.

Dealer or private sale
Is the seller the owner or a trader? Owners should have all the history and be happy to answer questions. Dealers may know less about a car, but should have some documentation, and may offer finance. In most countries, a dealer is required to ensure that the vehicle is 'fit for purpose,' which provides a safeguard should you find problems later. It's often worth paying a dealer's higher price for this peace of mind.

Cost of collection and delivery
Dealers may deliver, but it probably won't be cheap. Private owners may meet you halfway, especially if the car is roadworthy, but be sure to view the vehicle at the vendor's address beforehand to validate ownership and vehicle documentation.

Viewing – when and where?
It's essential to view the car at the vendor's address, and it that matches the name and address on the title documents – unless there's a good reason why not. Have at least one viewing in daylight during dry weather. Most cars look better in poor light or when wet.

Reason for sale
Genuine sellers will explain why they are selling and their length of ownership. They may also know something about previous owners.

Conversions and specials
Many TRs have returned to Europe from the USA. Conversion to RHD normally reduces its absolute value, but makes them more saleable in the UK. Conversion can be easily verified using the chassis number data in chapter 17. Check if the headlamps, wiper pattern, and side light colour are correct for your market, as some safety inspections insist on this. LHD cars also had differently wired side lights.

How you can pay
A cheque will take several days to clear, so the seller may prefer to sell to a cash buyer. Cash can also be a valuable bargaining tool. However, a banker's draft or money order may be as good as cash, so ask beforehand.

Condition (body/chassis/interior/mechanics)

Query the car's condition in the most specific terms as possible – preferably citing the checklist items described in chapter 9.

All original specification

Compared to a customised vehicle, an unmolested original car is invariably of a higher value, and is easier to source spares for.

Matching data/legal ownership/roadworthiness

All TRs have chassis, body, engine, and gearbox numbers, which should match to justify a top price. Although, changed engines, etc, that are noted on registration documents, are acceptable; especially if the original comes with the car.

Before buying, check if the car has any outstanding finance, is an insurance write-off or stolen, and has a consistent safety test certificate (MoT). In the UK, the following organisations can supply vehicle data (sometimes for a small fee):

DVSA 0300 123 9000   HPI 0845 300 8905   AA 0344 209 0754
DVLA 0844 306 9203   RAC 0330 159 0364

Other countries will have similar organisations. Search the internet for them.

Unleaded fuel

Modern fuel is quite aggressive compared to the fuel that these cars were designed to use. Ask if the engine has been converted to accept unleaded fuel, whether the metering unit (on a TR5) has been rebuilt with unleaded-compatible seals, and if the rubber fuel lines have been upgraded. Receipts should be available to prove all affirmative answers.

Insurance

If you intend to drive the car home, check with your existing insurer in case your current policy does not cover you. It's wise to check insurance costs before you purchase in any case – search 'classic car' insurance for suitable insurers in your area, and remember to ask for 'Agreed Value' insurance to ensure you have adequate cover.

Professional vehicle check

It's essential to thoroughly check over a car before you purchase it, especially from a private seller. If you feel unsure about making these checks yourself, many specialists will undertake a professional examination on your behalf, for a small fee (in the UK):

AA 0800 056 8040 (motoring organisation with vehicle inspectors)
RAC 0330 159 0720 (motoring organisation with vehicle inspectors)

The valves in this cylinder head have eroded the seats (arrowed). The cure is to fit modern hardened seats, making an unleaded engine. Check any engine rebuild invoices for this.

6 Inspection equipment

– these items will really help

It's essential to plan your inspection beforehand and take along the following items:

This book To be your guide at every step. Use the checkboxes in chapter 9 to help assess each area, and don't be afraid to let the seller see you using it.

A pen and notebook To record your observations and evaluation marks, see chapter 9.

Reading glasses (if needed) To read documents and make close up inspections.

A fridge or other magnet To check if the car has filler or fibreglass panels, but be careful not to damage the paintwork – it's best to wrap a thin layer of cloth around it. Chapters 7 and 9 highlight the locations to check.

A probe (such as a small screwdriver) To carefully prod any suspect areas, checking for rust, filler, or other horrors!

Overalls To keep you clean while under the car.

An old piece of carpet or cardboard Useful to lay on while under the car.

A torch To check the underside. Often you'll use it in conjunction with …

An adjustable mirror on a stick To check inaccessible areas – chapters 7 and 9 show where to look.

A digital camera or the camera in your phone To take reference photos of known trouble spots to study later, perhaps with the help of an expert.

A knowledgeable and enthusiastic friend To accompany you: a second opinion is invaluable and may stop your heart from ruling your head!

Optional extra equipment

If you can buy or borrow the following items without too much trouble, you'll be able to carry out a better inspection:

A trolley jack and two axle stands To raise the car off the ground one side or end at a time. Never go underneath a car that's supported only on a jack; put the axle stands under the chassis or suspension first.

A sparkplug spanner To check the state of tune of the engine by looking at the sparkplug colour and condition. While the plugs are out, why not use the next item …

An engine compression gauge To measure the compression pressure of each cylinder in turn while spinning the engine on the starter. A low reading on a cylinder indicates a defective or worn engine.

A combustion leakage tester To check if the head gasket is failing or if there's a crack in an engine casting. It fits on top of the radiator while the engine is ticking over to detect bubbles of exhaust gas.

A GPS Speedometer app On your phone to check the calibration of the speedometer while on your road test. (Safety first: never look at your phone whilst driving. Take a passenger to read the GPS speeds.)

(To purchase any of the first four items, go to your local auto factor or search online)

For inspections, jack the car on the chassis crossmember at the front (not the radiator protection panel), and the differential unit at the rear. Position the axle stands under the chassis or suspension: never on the body or sills. Never go underneath an inadequately supported car.

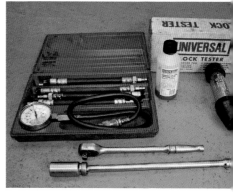

For a more thorough inspection, these are very useful: a compression gauge (in the red box), a block tester (to check for exhaust gases in the cooling system), and a sparkplug socket (foreground). You may find secondhand items for sale cheaply on eBay or similar sites.

7 Fifteen minute evaluation
– walk away or stay?

Caveat Emptor – Let the buyer beware! Remember, it's far easier not to buy a TR you have doubts about than to suppress those doubts and try to get a refund later!
- Don't let your heart rule your head.
- Be objective – difficult when looking at your dream classic car, but essential.
- Bring a level-headed friend with you and ask their opinion throughout the assessment process.

First impressions and gut feelings
If any of the following are true, walk away now:

Listen to your gut feeling
- Is the seller a bit too slick for an amateur?
- If the TR's being sold through a car dealership, before you visit, type its name into a search engine and see what customers say about it. Have a look around – does it look and feel professional, is it long established and trustworthy?

Paperwork
- Does the registration document match the seller's name and address?
- Have they owned the car for a short time without a good verifiable reason for its sale?
- Has it had lots of previous owners recently?
- Is there documentary proof of any explanations of discrepancies?

Price
- Is it too cheap for what's on offer?
- Is the seller pressuring you to buy with comments like "Other purchasers are arriving to view it soon!"
  If all is okay, it's time to move on to the 'Fifteen minute evaluation.'

Exterior
Assess the bodywork carefully:

1. Body symmetry Stand behind and in front of the car – does it look symmetrical? The tops of the wings have chrome strips on them that gently curve out around the cockpit area.
2. Paintwork Is it good? See chapter 14 for more details of what to look for.
3. Doors Look at the bottoms – is there a row of bubbles about 1cm above the bottom. If so, the skin has rusted through and will need replacing.
4. Wings Similarly, the rear edges of the front wings and the front edges of the rear wings also suffer from the 'row of bubbles' fault. If present, new panels are needed.

To check for body symmetry, stand back from the vehicle's bonnet and boot to see if the curves of the wing tops are equal. If not, suspect a poor quality restoration, or accident damage.

5. **Rear decking** The fuel filler protrudes through the central decking panel to which the forward and rear decking panels attach. Check for rust and filler along all edges and joints with your magnet.

6. **Rear body alignment** Stand at the back of the car and look beneath the bumper. The two rear chassis limb ends are partially visible beneath the rear valance panel. Is the same amount of chassis leg showing on each side? Less than 2cm difference is okay.

7. **Door gaps** Are the gaps consistent? Are the lower rear corners of each door not standing out proud from the rear wing?

8. **Bumpers** Are they rusty or dented?

9. **Windscreen frame** This removable frame often rusts out at the lower corners – bubbles and missing paint are the telltale signs. Is the frame painted body colour? (Only the TR6 had a satin black frame.)

10. **Soft top** Is it crease-free? Does it fold down nicely? Are the windows clear?

11. **Surrey top** Are both tops present, the metal panel top and the soft top, complete with support frame? Are they easy to install and remove? Has the soft top's corners shrunk? Are the top's securing thumb screws seized? If the chassis is in poor condition, the steel roof panel can end up supporting the car, do the doors function without the roof?

12. **Wheels**

    Wire wheels Rattle the blade of a screwdriver around the spokes and listen for an even ring? A dull thud means a loose spoke and a scrap wheel.

    All wheels Are the rims curbed? This is a symptom of bad and uncaring usage.

13. **Tyres**

    Tread depth In the UK, to be legal, it must have at least 1.6mm of tread depth across 75 per cent of the tread width.

    Size Are they all the same size (including the spare)? What size are they? The original tyre size is 165R15 on the TR4/4A/5 (meaning a 165mm tread width on

When checking rear body alignment, you are looking for how much of the rear chassis limb ends can be seen below the rear valance panel. The acceptable difference is less than 2cm.

These blisters on the lower rear wing indicate it is rusted through, and will likely need replacement.

The TR4/4A's chassis plate is located on the bulkhead panel at the rear of the engine bay. It includes two-digit colour codes for the body paint and the interior trim.

The TR5/250's engine number is stamped on the block between number five and six sparkplugs (counting from the front).

The TR5/250 chassis plate is located under the bonnet on the left-hand wheelarch. This yellow car was originally painted 'New White (19).' The trim should be 'Matador Red (12),' see chapter 17.

COMM N° XXXXXX
PAINT 19 TRIM 12
GROSS LADEN WEIGHT LBS
MANUFACTURED BY
THE STANDARD TRIUMPH MOTOR C? LTD.
COVENTRY, ENGLAND.

a 15in rim with the default 82 per cent aspect ratio of sidewall height to tread width) and 185R15 on the TR250. An acceptable alternative is 185/70R15 on the TR4/4A/5 (a wider 185mm tread with a 70 per cent aspect ratio) and 205/70R15 on the TR250. If larger, check they don't foul the suspension or wheelarches on full lock and full suspension travel.

The TR4/4A's engine number is stamped on the engine block under sparkplug three (counting from the front, of course).

Tyre age Most tyres have a date stamp on the sidewall – a four-digit number in an oval cartouche – for example, '2312' means a tyre made in week 23 of 2012. Are any older than seven years? Are the sidewalls cracked?

This tyre was manufactured in week 49 (December) of 2016.

14. Doors, bonnet, and boot lid Do they all open and close correctly? Misalignment and poor catches can make this difficult. A simple realignment is usually the cure, but be wary of bigger problems such as adjacent panels too close for adequate clearance. Check the corners of the bonnet aren't bent upwards – this happens when the bonnet release cable breaks and a misguided owner tries to lever the bonnet open with a large screwdriver.

Under the bonnet

Open the bonnet and have a look:

1. Engine bay cleanliness Is this in keeping with the rest of the car and honest-looking? Is it painted the same colour as the exterior paintwork?
2. Chassis number and engine number Check these against the data in chapter 17. If the engine number has a different prefix from what you were expecting, this usually means the engine has come from a saloon car and may be detuned.
3. Paint and trim colour codes These are on the chassis plate. Do the codes agree with the actual colours?
4. Engine fluids
   Engine oil Pull out the dipstick and have a look. Is it about the right level? What colour is it? Black means it's old. Creamy white means it has water in it, possibly from a leaking gasket.
   Radiator coolant Remove the radiator cap. Is the level right? Is there evidence of antifreeze? Is it a brownish colour? If so, this may indicate that sealant has been added to plug a leak.
   Brake and clutch fluids Remove the master cylinder caps, check these are at maximum, and are not cloudy or dirty in appearance.

5. **Left- or right-hand drive conversion** Look at the horizontal bulkhead panel on the passenger side next to the battery (TR4/4A), or the vertical panel in front of it (TR5/250). Has it been replaced with a simple flat panel? The correct panels have indented patterns (swages) to reduce vibration. If it's flat, it's likely a replacement. A converted car is worth less than one that isn't – see chapter 4 'Relative values.'

Underneath

Lift the car up as much as possible and see what you can:

1. **Chassis** The IRS chassis (TR4A/5/250) suffers from corrosion problems in front of the differential. There, the 'T-shirt' panel (because it's shaped like one!), joins four main chassis limbs. Rust gets between the steel layers and causes bulges and holes. Check all over the chassis (TR4/4A/5/250) for rust damage, poor repairs, and accident damage evidence.
2. **Drips under the engine, gearbox, and back axle** A few drips are usual, but an oil slick large enough to be environmentally notifiable is bad news!
3. **Brake fluid leakage** Check all brake hoses and the inside lower sidewalls of the tyres for evidence of this.

Cockpit

1. **Seats** Are they comfortable? If they're very saggy, it means the seat foams and rubber diaphragms are very old.
2. **Handbrake** Note the TR4 has a floor mounted fly-off handbrake, whereas, in the TR4A/TR5/TR250, it's on the tunnel between the seats (as described in chapter 3). Does it work, without sticking?
3. **Dashboard** On the TR4, it's painted metal, whereas on other models it is veneered wood. If it's wooden, is it faded by the sun or chipped and unsightly?

Driving

Now it's time to fire the engine up and see how it drives:

1. **Cold starting** The engine will need full choke from cold, but should start promptly without excessive churning on the starter. It should start on all cylinders and run cleanly and evenly. The fuel-injected TR5s often start on five cylinders, taking a few minutes before running cleanly on all six – a not uncommon quirk you can ignore.
2. **Exhaust smoke** If there's any smoke, what colour is it?
   Blue smoke Means the engine is burning oil and is likely badly worn.
   Black smoke Means excess petrol – maybe the choke needs to go back in.
   A little white smoke Just means steam – quite normal and nothing to worry about while the exhaust system is cold. Significant amounts of steam when thoroughly hot might indicate a blown head gasket, etc.
   Thick white smoke Means burning brake fluid. This can only happen on the TR5/250 and other cars with a brake servo. Urgent attention is required.
3. **Radiator** With the engine ticking over, remove the radiator cap (be very careful as it can be hot). The water should be moving, indicating the pump is working. If it bubbles a lot, this may indicate a blown head gasket.

4. **Oil pressure** Keep a note of this at all times. The pressure should start at 60-80psi, and when thoroughly hot after a lengthy run, it should drop to no less than 50psi at about 2000rpm. Readings less than this can have a number of causes, but might indicate a worn engine.

5. **Clutch** With first gear engaged, this should take up the drive smoothly. If it judders, there may be loose engine mounts or oil on the clutch, indicating a leak from the rear crank seal. Check for clutch slip when driving uphill, indicated by an unexpected rise in engine revs.

6. **Stability** On the road, the car should not pull noticeably to one side or the other. Veering in the direction of the road camber is not unusual as these cars don't have power steering. Cornering should be reassuringly positive with no attendant noises of rubbing, etc.

7. **Brakes** The car should pull up square. The handbrake should hold the vehicle on an incline.

8. **Overdrive** If fitted, it shouldn't slip under load, similar to the clutch above. See chapter 3 for more details on how to use the overdrive.

9. **Smoke on the overrun** When the engine is thoroughly warm, accelerate up to a reasonable speed and lift your foot off the accelerator, looking in the mirror as the car slows under engine braking. Can you see any blue smoke? This means engine wear.

Paperwork

Have another look at the paperwork. After reading chapter 11, you should know what paperwork to expect. In the 'First impressions' section on p19, you've checked whether the name and address describe the seller and the location of the car.

The registration document should agree with the chassis and engine numbers. Does the build date tally with the 'Production dates' tables in the 'Vital statistics' section of chapter 17? If not, the car may have been imported.

Is there a safety inspection certificate? In the UK, cars over 40 years old don't need one, although it's advisable to have one to prove the car is truly roadworthy. If present, is it current and not about to expire? Never be fobbed off by a seller telling you that a car without one would pass the test easily – what are they hiding?

Conclusion – is it worth a more thorough look?

1. Stand back, take a deep breath, and compare notes with your friend.
   - Is the car comfortable for you to sit in and drive?
   - Is it noisier or coarser than you could live with?
   - Is it the only car of this model that you've driven? If so, you have nothing to compare it with.
   - Is the colour something you can live with? (Caution – colour changes are not cheap. If it has to be a particular colour, then go and find one that colour.)

2. Are any shortcomings you've noted reflected in the price? Are they potentially deal-breakers because they could be expensive to fix?

3. Did you find anything that suggests a less than 100 per cent honest description in the advert? Does the seller 'feel' honest? What's your gut feeling about the whole situation?

4. Remember, let the buyer beware. If in any doubt, walk away with your money still in your pocket.
   If it's a case of 'so far, so good', move on to the 'Serious Evaluation' (chapter 9).

Beware of a row of rust bubbles near the edge of a panel, such as on this TR4a bonnet. When the panel was cut open ...

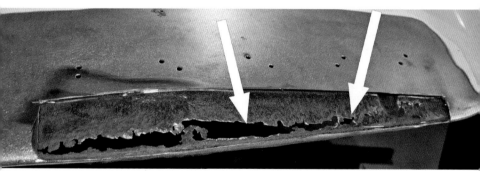

... this is what was behind. The inner frame had also rusted through. Like the proverbial iceberg, it's what's below the surface that you have to worry about.

The rear decking panel is very prone to rust damage and subsequent poor repairs. Check these joints carefully, both inside and outside the boot.

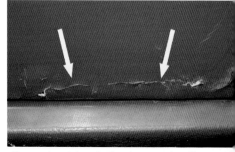

Trapped moisture in the doors makes the skins rust through, appearing in a line of paint bubbles and cracks about 1cm above the bottom edges. This door skin is scrap.

Surface rust like this on the rear chassis limb hasn't significantly weakened the chassis yet. But it indicates a lack of maintenance by the owner.

An example of a poor door gap: it's too wide and tapers in towards the bottom. The bottom corner may also stand proud of the adjacent rear wing surface.

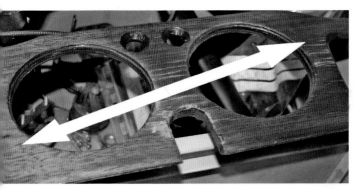

The TR4A/5/250 wooden dashboards fade if exposed to extreme sunlight or damp conditions. Note the differences in colour between the two areas.

Oh dear, this TR4A engine bay is in a very sorry state! A lot of cleaning, painting, and general restoration will be needed to get it looking good again.

If your prospective purchase has passed the 'Fifteen minute evaluation' in chapter 7, it now needs a more serious inspection before you're tempted to negotiate a deal.

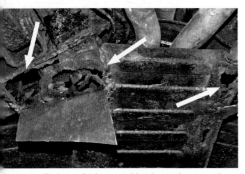

Bulges, holes, and bad patches on the T-shirt panel, in front of the differential, (TR4A/5/250) can have bad corrosion like this in the chassis limbs underneath.

The trailing arm limbs (TR4A/5/250) rust out near the suspension bracket bolt holes.

This chassis limb has cracked due to stress, and possibly internal rust. A careful inspection of the chassis is necessary to spot such faults.

Pay for a professional inspection?

As mentioned in chapter 5, it's essential to thoroughly check over a car before making a purchase, especially from a private seller. If you feel unsure about making these checks yourself, many specialists will undertake a professional examination on your behalf for a small fee, maybe at a professional workshop. They also usually provide the reassurance of indemnity insurance should they miss significant faults. Search 'classic car inspection' for a list of local specialists, and ask if they have such insurance. If the seller refuses an inspection, what are they trying to hide?

Or undertake your own inspection

You'll likely not remember every detail of your serious inspection, even an hour or two later, so have your pen (or pencil) ready and tick the excellent (4), good (3), average (2), or poor (1) boxes in each section as you go along. The totting up procedure is detailed at the end of the chapter. Be realistic in your marking – it'll pay dividends in the long run.

The inspection will follow a logical order starting in a vital area.

Underneath

Firstly, jack the car up at the front, securing it safely with axle stands. Later, jack the rear up similarly (or, better still, borrow/hire a car lift).

Chassis

Inspect it carefully, from front to rear. You are looking for:

1. Severe rust damage Especially where chassis limbs overlap. Are any parts of the chassis bulging outwards or holed? On IRS cars, the rear corners of the 'T-shirt' area, just in front of the differential unit and the two trailing arm limbs (where the rear suspension brackets are bolted), are areas of concern.

2. Areas of poor repairs Are any existing repairs of good quality, welded all around the repair patches, and strong-looking? If rust is streaking out anywhere or if a weld consists of lots of small blobs of metal (what professional restorers call 'Pigeon Sh*t'!), then it needs redoing.

3. Distortions and creases Has the car been in an accident, evidenced by creases in the otherwise flat surfaces of the chassis limbs? For example, a frontal impact on a wheel will usually distort or crease the main chassis limb behind the point of impact. Sometimes these are disguised with filler or body lead, use your magnet if it looks suspicious.

4. Lots of surface rust Is this present? It indicates a general lack of maintenance and care.

5. Missing reinforcements on IRS chassis Have the extra brackets been welded to the front suspension lower mounting brackets to support through the outer and upper chassis surfaces? Are the front differential support pin mounts boxed in on the inner faces of the spring crossmember above the differential? A broken pin mount drops the differential a bit, causing a telltale 'thump' from the rear when pulling away.

6. Cracks Check for cracks and fretting, especially around all mounting points.

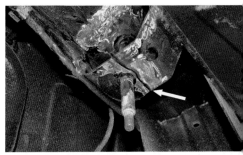

The right-hand front differential mounting pin (TR4A/5/250) is always the first to crack. It needs welding and reinforcing to prevent it happening again.

This IRS chassis (TR4A/5/250) has had the front differential support brackets welded and reinforced by boxing in the sides.

Extra brackets (TR4A/5/250) strengthen the lower front suspension support brackets to prevent flexing and cracking, and are essential!

Front suspension,  brakes, and steering
Inspect these carefully. You are looking for:

1. Worn suspension bushes Are the rubber bushes perished and cracked? (The best bushes are polyurethane and usually not black.)
2. Rust areas around nuts and bolts Are there telltale rust streaks, indicating a bolt is loose and moving? The main culprit here is usually the main through bolt in the front suspension lower trunion.
3. Damaged shock absorbers and springs Do any shock absorbers leak? Are any springs broken?
4. Badly worn brakes Can you see any of the following: leaking brake fluid, cracked flexible hoses, worn out brake pads, and badly scored discs?
5. Worn steering parts Is there play in the trackrod end ball joints, torn steering rack gaiters, play in the rack mounts or oil leaking from the rack?
6. Front wheel bearings Grab hold of each front tyre at top and bottom and rock it in and out. Is there excessive play? Spin each wheel by hand – does it 'rumble'?

Polyurethane suspension bushes (brightly coloured) are better and longer lasting than rubber ones.

Rear suspension and brakes
Inspect these carefully. You are looking for:

1. Worn suspension bushes On the TR4, are the rear shackle bushes perished? On the IRS cars, are the large trailing arm bushes perished?
2. Damaged shock absorbers and springs If fitted, are the lever arm shockers leaking? Have telescopic

This TR5/250 rolling chassis has the differential, suspension, steering, fuel, and brake pipes fitted. It's ready to receive the engine, gearbox, and newly painted bodyshell.

The TR4 chassis has a live back axle and semi-elliptic rear springs. The main chassis limbs are widely spaced apart under the axle, making it stronger than the IRS chassis.

shocker (and optional brackets) been fitted? Are the leaf springs (TR4) or coil springs (IRS) broken?

3. Rear wheel bearings On the TR4, is there any play or leakage of axle oil? On IRS cars, is there any play whatsoever in the rear hub bearings? Even the slightest movement of the tyre when rocked means the bearing is scrap.

4. Brakes Is there any leaking brake fluid? Are the flexible hoses cracked? Are the fixed pipes rusted or kinked? Are the handbrake cable(s) in good order?

Engine, gearbox, 4 3 2 1
propshaft and rear differential unit, driveshafts (IRS or rear axle TR4)
Inspect the undersides. You are looking for:

1. Excessive oil leaks All these cars drip a bit. The joke goes, when they stop dripping, they've run out! However, are there large puddles, and is excessive oil streaking down the chassis underside?

2. Engine and gearbox mounts Are these sagging or cracked?

3. Propshaft Grip the shaft and flange on each side of the UJs, twisting back and forth. Can you feel any free play?

4. Driveshafts (IRS cars) Do the four universal joints (UJs) suffer from play, just like the propshaft UJs? Are the sliding spline joints showing excessive play, causing them to 'clonk' in use?

Fuel and brake 4 3 2 1
pipes, and exhaust system
You are looking for:

1. Damaged fuel and brake pipes Are any leaking, kinked or corroded?

2. Exhaust system Is the exhaust stainless steel and therefore rust

In contrast, the main chassis limbs at the rear of the IRS chassis narrow to give enough room for the rear suspension trailing arms. This gives better roadholding and ride, at the expense of a slightly weaker and more rust-prone chassis.

Look out for scoring on both sides of the discs. This scoring isn't too bad. Deep scoring or heavy rust damage means disc renewal.

This IRS trailing arm limb and bracket are heavily rusted, and the trailing arm bush is in need of renewal (arrowed). Cleaning off the rust may reveal chassis cracks and rust holes.

free? Are there any leaks, damaged silencers, broken or missing mounts? Does it foul the chassis anywhere?

Lower bodywork
You are looking for:

1. Rust damage Are there areas of rust damage or unsightly and poor repair patches? Is any underseal missing?
2. Accident damage Is any visible? (Check also inside the wheelarches for damage not visible from the outside.)

Now you can let the car down onto the ground again.

Wheels and tyres
Assess using the information in chapter 7. Inspect everything closely, including the spare, look for bulges in sidewalls, cuts, or other damage.

Bodywork, paintwork, and brightwork

Now inspect all of the car's bodywork closely with your eyes and your hands! The latter are incredibly sensitive at detecting incorrect panel shapes, dents, and even some paint defects that the eye often doesn't see. Remember that artificial light often reveals more distortions and colour mismatch problem than natural daylight.

Bodywork
Inspect all the body panels using your eyes, hands, and a magnet. You are looking for:

1. Overall body shape Stand back from the body and assess the symmetry, curves, and overall shape from all angles. While this won't be up to the perfection of a modern car, it should be pretty good. At the back of the car, look at the rear ends of the two main chassis limbs that are partially visible below the rear valance – are

The driveshafts on IRS cars (TR4A/5/250) can wear, causing clonks and vibration. Note this car has the better (yellow) polyurethane front differential mounts and trailing arm bushes. The rear differential mounts are still rubber.

'165R15' is the normal tyre size for non-USA cars. '86' is the load rating – 530kg max. 'H' is a speed rating of 130mph max – more than adequate. This tyre is of the correct size.

Tyres over about seven years old suffer from hardened rubber, which results in a lack of grip. Many tyres have a manufacturing date stamp. This tyre was made in week 49 (December) of 2016.

they visible to an equal amount on each side? Asymmetry of less than 2cm is okay (See picture on page 20).

2. Rust damage Rust forms in joints between two pieces of metal where water can be trapped, so it's mostly found near the edges and joins of panels. Inspect the following areas closely:

a. Front valance edges Look inside the wheelarches at the bolted joints and the outside of the valance.

b. The rear of front wings The trailing edge of the wings rusts about 1cm in from the rear edge due to an internal flange. The bottoms of the wings rust badly because the sill extensions behind them are very close, and the areas are fed with water from the bulkhead drain pipes above! The splash panels inside the wheelarches often rust badly. The top wing edges adjacent to the scuttle rust too.

c. Windscreen frame Check the bottom corners.

d. Doors Open the doors and feel the thickness of the door skin lower flanges by running your thumb and forefinger along the lower edge, one digit outside and the other inside. The flange should be parallel, with a cross-section like a letter 'U'. If however, it feels like the letter 'V', rust has pushed the seam open, and paint bubbles will appear soon. (Be very careful doing this as jagged edges of metal inside the door could cut you.) Assess the panel gaps around the doors, especially near the lower rear corner, which often stick out proud of the wing.

e. Sills Are the lower edges badly rusted? Be aware that thick black underseal is often used as camouflage here.

To test for broken spokes on a wire wheel, gently tap each spoke in turn with a metal instrument, such as a screwdriver; they should ring. A dull thud means a broken or loose thread and the wheel is scrap.

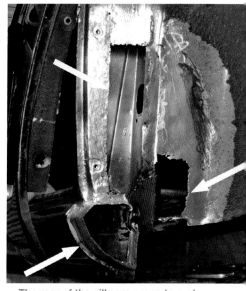

The rear of the sills are prone to rust damage. The sill's end cap has been cut away, revealing damage to the inner (bottom left arrow). The rear of B-pillar has rusted through and been cut away for repair (top arrow). The rear floor corner has rusted away (bottom right arrow) next to the seat belt mount reinforcement (painted in red primer).

f. Floor pans Are the floors rust damaged? Check at the front by the inner sills, behind by the rear door pillar, and round all the edges.

g. Rear wings Look for similar defects to the front wings. The top edge near the rear decking join is another problem area. Inspect the boot from inside with your torch.

h. Rear decking This suffers badly from rust damage along the joins. Look inside the boot at the inner welded joins – they're often a frightful sight!

i. Boot lid Is this rusting along the lower edge where condensation gathers inside? Is the fit of this panel too tight along the sides? Is the lock difficult to operate?

j. Rear valance Look for similar damage to the front valance – you know the drill now!

3. Accident damage Looking inside the wings might well reveal accident damaged panels that are disguised on the outside. Use your magnet over all of the body panels to look for areas of filler covering over dents, etc. The magnet should have a consistent attraction over all areas.

4. Non-steel panel Are all of the panels steel? (Use your magnet.) Fibreglass is bad news, aluminium maybe good news as this was used in motorsport for lightness.

Paintwork
4 3 2 1

Check by looking at and feeling all body panels. The paint should be a beautiful flat and shiny surface, as well as a consistent colour. The ten types of defect you are looking for are described in chapter 14.

Chrome brightwork
4 3 2 1

This means the chrome bumpers, door handles, etc. Are any items, especially the bumpers, bent, dented, or rust damaged? Are the chrome Mazak items (door handles, boot handles, along with the front and rear light bezels) corroded with small pits all over?

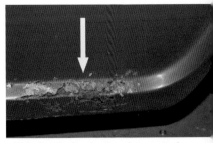

This front wing bottom has rusted through because of the wet debris trapped between it and the sill panel behind. Both will require renewal.

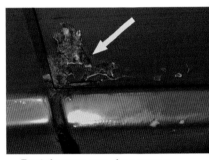

Rust damage on a door corner (arrow) means a new skin at the very least. The row of bubbles to the right of this area and about 1cm up from the bottom are caused by rust holes through the skin.

With the rear wing removed, heavy rust damage to the inner wing and forward decking arm edge can often be seen (left arrow). There's also rust damage to the rear of the B-pillar (right arrow).

Under the bonnet

Open the bonnet and have a good look around.

General engine   bay assessment
Assess the following items:

1. Corrosion damage
   a. Rust damage around the rear bulkhead Is it rusted behind and below the battery? Water inside the bulkhead drainage cavity and battery acid cause the problems here
   b. Corrosion on the battery terminals Is there any white furry powder?
   c. Rust damage around the inner arch seams Where the front wheels throw water at them.
   d. Rust damage (low down beneath the brake master cylinder and wiper motor) There are body mounts here, and the rust gets in amongst the reinforcements.
2. Untidiness If it looks a bit like Tracey Emin's bed, then clearly there's been some neglect! And if it's the wrong paint colour, then be aware, rectifying this will entail stripping out the whole engine bay to respray it.
3. Wiring loom There's a fair amount of wiring loom under the bonnet, and it should be secured neatly using the metal tangs on the body with no chafing. View areas of unsightly repair with concern as wiring can catch fire very easily if it's been bodged. Look out for any ScotchLoks or similar insulation-displacement loom extenders – they are nothing but trouble in the long-term, and are used by amateurs when proper wiring connectors are not available. Beware!
4. Chassis and engine numbers It's very important that these agree with what's recorded in the documentation. The 'Vital Statistics' section in chapter 17 tells you what to expect for the model and year of car you're looking at. If the chassis number doesn't agree with the documentation, walk away now as there may be

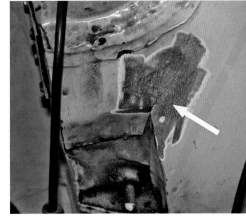

Check carefully for cracks in the body: this one is on the bulkhead.

The windscreen frame often rusts in the bottom corners. This shot-blasted frame has extensive rust damage and a large block of filler (arrowed). All that showed on the outside were rust holes next to the screen seal.

a fraudulent reason for this. If the engine number doesn't agree, this isn't serious, as many cars have had exchange engines fitted during their lifetime. Be aware that the wrong engine number prefix usually means it's from a Triumph saloon, and may well still be de-tuned – unless you see full documentary proof to the contrary.

5. RHD/LHD conversion Clue one: Factory left-hand drive cars have an 'L' suffix on their chassis numbers (chapter 17). Clue two: Look at the master cylinder support panel beside the battery on the passenger side – it's horizontal on the TR4/4A and vertical on the TR5/250. Has it been replaced with a simple flat panel? The correct panel has noticeable indented swage pressings to reduce vibration, and is spot welded in. If it's perfectly flat and/or there is visible evidence of welding, it's likely a replacement covering the master cylinder holes. A converted car is less valuable than one that isn't – see chapter 4.

Mechanical 4 3 2 1
evaluation

Assess the engine properly, taking your time and looking carefully. You are looking for:

1. Oil on the dipstick The dipstick is on the left-hand side of the engine in all cases. The oil on it should be near the MAX line (assuming the car is parked on the level), and reasonably clean. Very low oil may well mean high oil consumption. Very black oil indicates poor maintenance. Creamy mayonnaise-coloured oil suggests there's water mixed in with it. This is especially important on the four-cylinder engines (TR4/4A), which have 'wet' cylinder liners. These liners sit on a pair of 'figure-of-eight'

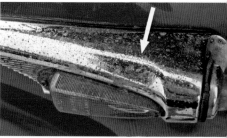

This chromed front sidelight unit is made of Mazak, which corrodes by forming little pits of oxide on its surface. Renewal is needed.

The bulkhead under the battery, steering column, and master cylinders often rusts, especially if contaminated with battery acid and brake fluid. Here, a new panel is about to be fitted.

Spilt brake fluid causes this rust damage underneath the master cylinders. A strip and repaint is needed at the very least; maybe even a new panel, too, if rust damage is bad.

seals in the block, which are prone to corrosion damage and leakage. Correcting this fault generally requires a full engine rebuild.

2. Oil filter Located low down on the left-hand side of the engine. Both engines had a sideways mounted renewable element filter. Is there evidence of leaks? If a modern spin-on conversion is fitted, this is very desirable.

3. Engine cleanliness Does the engine look neat and tidy? Oil streaks and rust are signs of neglect and wear.

4. Cooling system Are all the hoses in good order, not cracked, or worn away by adjacent objects? Is the radiator core consistent in appearance with no damaged or missing cooling fins? Are there any drips under the water pump, the hoses, the radiator, the heater valve on the right-hand side of the engine? Does the coolant have antifreeze in it (an antifreeze strength tester can be purchased quite cheaply)? If an electric fan is fitted, does it spin freely, and has it been mounted in a secure way close to the radiator core?

5. Engine cylinder compressions Are all the cylinders working equally in providing power for a smooth performance? The easiest way to assess this is with a compression gauge set. This inexpensive tool provides a reading of the peak compression pressure in each cylinder. Remove all the sparkplugs, screw the gauge into number one cylinder (nearest the radiator) and spin the engine over on the starter motor until the gauge will read no

In the engine bay, check this body support point on the chassis diagonal member, next to the distributor (left side), and the manifolds (right side). This is the result of rust damage between the bodywork panels ...

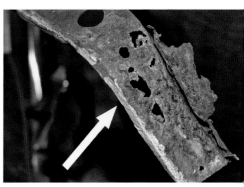

... when the upper panel is removed, this rust damage can be seen. The large circular hole at the top is where the body mounting bolt goes through; the other holes shouldn't be there!

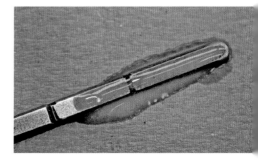

If the oil on the engine dipstick looks like this, beware! Water mixed with oil causes a creamy, mayonnaise-coloured mixture. There's likely to be a blown gasket or a cracked casting. New oil is clear and pale, going blacker with use; it's never creamy.

higher. Take a note of the pressure reached, and repeat for each of the other cylinders, one at a time. Look for a consistency of numbers across all the cylinders, rather than a particular pressure reading value. A range of 20 per cent is acceptable. A low reading on a cylinder suggests a burnt out valve or broken piston ring, etc.

6. Sparkplugs While they're out, have a look at the sparkplug ends. Are they clean with no excessive deposits and dark grey in colour? Light grey means too little fuel, black means too much, and black wetness means oil contamination from a worn engine (and usually blue smoke).

7. Brake and clutch master cylinders Remove the lids from the two master cylinders and check the fluid. It should be at or near the MAX line and be clean. Yellow fluid generally means a normal DOT3, DOT4, or DOT5.1 glycol fluid is being used, whereas purple fluid generally means it's a silicone (DOT5) fluid. Use of the latter is controversial: many like it as it doesn't absorb atmospheric moisture (non-hygroscopic), nor blister paintwork if spilt. Whereas others dislike the slightly spongy feel it often gives to the braking system. Most owners favour DOT4 or DOT5.1, which are much less hygroscopic and kinder to paintwork than DOT3.

8. Fuel lines, throttle linkages, etc Are all the fuel lines in good order with no kinks, cracks, corrosion, or leaks, and are not routed too close to the exhaust manifold, water pump pulley,

A modern spin-on oil filter conversion is fitted in place of the original canister type. This good modification makes oil changes easier.

All the sparkplugs should be a dark grey/brown colour. Black, too rich; white, too lean; wetness equals oil burning equals a worn out engine!

An engine compression gauge will tell you a lot about the engine. Look for similar readings across all cylinders rather than a particular reading. Remove all the sparkplugs first so that the engine turns over faster on the starter.

etc? Do the throttle linkages operate freely without stickiness?

9. Exhaust manifold This was originally a robust cast iron item. Often it has been replaced by a fabricated 'bunch of bananas' multi-pipe extractor manifold, which gives worthwhile extra performance at the expense of being noisier. In either case, is it free of cracks and visible leaks (often evidenced by telltale black soot marks)? Are all studs and flanges intact and not cracked or broken?

This 4-into-1 'bunch of bananas' manifold on a TR4/4A is a desirable performance modification.

10. Engine mounts These 2 are on either side of the engine, low down at the front. Are they free of cracks and not saggy? Do they support the engine well and restrict the engine from rocking from side to side under acceleration?

11. Wiper motor and washer system Do these work okay? The TR5/250 has a two-speed wiper motor. The washer system often leaks or gets blocked if neglected.

12. Modern unleaded fuel issues These cars date from the days of benign leaded fuel. Today's petrol will erode the exhaust valve seats in the engine unless they have been replaced by hardened valve seat inserts – has it been converted? On the TR5 PI, the metering unit will suffer from leaking seals if it hasn't been rebuilt recently with modern more robust seals – is it unleaded compatible? Are the rubber fuel lines compatible with aggressive modern fuel that cracks older rubber ones? Ask to see documentary evidence that all these items are okay.

13. Crankshaft end float On all cars, the crankshaft thrust washers (which resist the forward push on the crankshaft when the clutch pedal is depressed) are only just adequate. If they have worn badly, or, worse still, fallen into the sump, an expensive rebuild beckons. Assess this by using a large screwdriver (or similar lever) to move the front crankshaft pulley back and forward as far as it will go. Does it move more than a few thousandths of an inch – about the thickness of a page of this book? (Driving tip: to avert thrust washer failure, never sit with your foot on the clutch pedal when stationary or in a traffic jam.)

Inside the car

Now it's time to assess the cockpit area. Inspect the following:

Check the crankshaft end float using a large screwdriver or pry bar, levering the crankshaft nose backwards and forwards against the chassis cross tube. The free play must not exceed 0.006in – roughly the thickness of a page of this book.

If the seat is saggy, this rubber diaphragm has probably split, and the foam behind it is crumbling. These parts can easily be renewed, but it's a bargaining point.

1. The general condition of the trim Is the cockpit a nice place to be, tidy, with a pleasant ambience? If it is a bit tatty, but the car is otherwise sound, it probably would be a good buy at the right price. However, a superb interior in a rusty and otherwise poor vehicle is as much use as a new roof on a dilapidated house: it's best avoided!

2. Dashboard and instruments The TR4 has a white painted dashboard, while the TR4A/5/250 has a wooden one. If fitted, is the wood faded or cracked from bright sunlight or mistreatment? Are the instruments a matched original set? Are the dash top padding and lower padded crash pads cracked or wrinkled?

3. Seats Do these suffer from cracked, split, or faded seat covers? Is there collapsed interior foam (often shown by yellow foam powder under the seats), broken lower rubber diaphragms underneath, or broken internal steel frame limbs? Note that some cars are fitted with more modern seats from, for example, the Mazda MX5. These detract from the originality, but are preferred by some owners for their increased comfort and support. If upgraded seats are fitted, are the originals also included in the deal?

4. Carpets Are these suffering from general wear and tear? Are the upper surfaces faded by sunlight?

5. Side trims These are fitted to the doors, footwell sides, rear sides, and the central side areas. Are they a matched set, colour coordinated with the seats and not ripped, tatty, or warped by water ingress behind?

6. H-frame This straddles the gearbox cover just in front of the gearlever. You might think it's there just to provide a home for the radio, but actually, its main job is to stop the dashboard shaking over rough terrain (the dreaded 'scuttle shake'). Is it firmly bolted in all four corners and not broken? The radio's speakers are often housed in 'kidney panels' on either side – if present, are these firmly fixed?

7. Soft top, soft top bag, and tonneau cover If fitted, the soft top is fully removable on the TR4, and permanently attached across the

A tatty cockpit is another bargaining point. New trim kits and carpet sets are readily available.

rear deck on the TR4A/5/250. In the latter case, it folds down easily, but must be folded in the correct way to avoid damage to the rear window prior to being covered with the storage bag (See online videos of how to do this). When down, the tonneau cover can be fitted to cover the whole cockpit area. Are all these items in good order, easy to fit and remove, without tears or fading, and with all the securing poppers present and in working order?

The H-frame in the cockpit (shaped like a large capital 'H'!) prevents the dashboard from shaking over a bumpy road, and houses the radio and a few switches.

8. Surrey top This desirable optional extra replaces the normal soft top with a glass rear window in an aluminium frame. (Porsche's Targa Top is a copy of this). The roof section is either a steel panel or a fabric panel supported on a fold-away frame. Are both roofs present and in good working order? Are the corner poppers on the fabric roof working, or is there fabric shrinkage? Try them all to see that they're working.

9. Boot Is there a usable spare wheel that isn't illegal, flat, or the wrong size (check it actually fits the car)? Is there a wheel nut spanner (steel wheels) or a copper hide mallet (wire wheels) present? Is there a jack – preferably a scissor jack and handle? (The original jack operates

Old wooden dashboards on the TR4A/5/250 crack and discolour.

through a large grommet in each floor and is pretty useless!) If octagonal wire wheel spinners are fitted, is there a large spanner for them. Is the boot correctly lined with trimboards (front and both sides), baseboard (over the spare wheel) and a carpet?

Driving the car

For a test drive, you'll need insurance cover and the car will need to be road legal. The owner will have to drive you if insurance is a problem.

Start-up

There's a lot to take note of in the first start-up so familiarise yourself beforehand with what to look for.

1. Systems test Before starting the engine, test the side and headlights, indicators, stop lights, horn, wipers, washers, and seatbelts. Are they all working?

2. Ignition on Does the red ignition light come on and the fuel gauge slowly rise? With the TR5, can you hear the PI pump in the boot emitting a suppressed hum (and hopefully nothing louder)? Originally, the other models had a manual fuel pump, which might need priming to aid starting if the car hasn't been used for a few days – it's on the left-hand side of the engine, with the priming lever underneath. Check that the gear lever is in neutral and the handbrake is on.

The TR4 soft top stows in the boot, and the frame folds inside these vinyl covers, leaving room on the back seat. In contrast, the TR4A/5/250 roof folds onto the back seat, leaving very little room.

3. Start-up Pull the choke fully out and twist it a quarter turn clockwise to lock it in position. Operate the starter on the ignition key. Does the engine start promptly, perhaps with a little push on the accelerator pedal? Does it settle down after a few seconds to achieve smooth running? Note that the TR5's fuel-injected engine often starts on only five cylinders. This is due to an injector having a small trapped air bubble which usually clears after a few seconds. If present, does the misfire clear after a few minutes so that the engine runs cleanly on all six cylinders?

   a. Oil pressure gauge It must rise promptly to over 50psi.

   b. Revs Adjust the choke inwards to stabilise this at about 1500rpm.

   c. Exhaust smoke If there's smoke, what colour is it?

      • Blue smoke Means the engine is burning oil, indicating wear.

      • Black smoke Means excess petrol – maybe the choke needs pushing in.

      • Thin white smoke Means steam – quite normal and nothing to worry about while the exhaust system is cold. Significant amounts of steam when thoroughly hot might indicate a blown head gasket, etc.

      • Thick white smoke Means burning brake fluid. This only happens on the TR5/250 and any cars with a brake servo. Urgent attention is required.

   d. Noise Keep an ear open for unusual noises from the engine and exhaust system. It should be reasonably quiet with a consistent gentle mechanical noise. A pronounced 'clacking' noise indicates a badly adjusted tappet at the very least, and maybe a more serious problem.

Driving   4   3   2   1

Choose a route that includes, if possible, slow urban traffic jams, hills, bumpy roads, and high-speed motorways to test the full range of the car's capabilities.

The optional Surrey top comes with a steel roof such as this. There's no room to stow it in the car, so it's for winter use ...

During the drive, don't forget to push the choke back in (if used for a cold start) and pay close attention to the following points:

... however, the fabric roof is stowed in the boot with its foldable frame and can be erected in just a few minutes.

1. Engine noise Are there any unusual engine noises, especially when pulling hard. Rattling often indicates bearing trouble. A light metallic sound (pinking) usually indicates tuning problems and low octane fuel. (All these cars must use premium grade fuel.)
2. Gearbox Is there good synchromesh on all forward gears, or do any 'graunch' when going into gear? Are quick changes up and down carried out smoothly?
4. Overdrive If fitted, there'll be a long lever on the side of the steering column (or perhaps an aftermarket switch on the gearlever). Get the car up to about 50mph, glance at the speedo and tacho to make a mental note of the two readings, lift off the accelerator slightly to give a 'neutral' throttle (neither accelerating nor decelerating), and operate the overdrive switch. Do the revs immediately drop a few hundred rpm while the speed stays constant? Now accelerate quite hard – is the overdrive slipping and allowing the revs to rise with no speed increase. Now, again on a 'neutral' throttle, disengage the overdrive. Do the revs promptly increase again? Repeat the whole procedure in third and second gears at a suitable road speed for each. Second gear overdrive is the severest test as lower road speeds show up a worn and slipping overdrive more easily.
5. Brakes Do these pull up smoothly and in a straight line on a flat road? (However, a slight pull towards the gutter on a heavily cambered road is okay.) Is there 'juddering' under braking, as felt through the steering wheel and indicative of a distorted disc or drum?
6. Steering Is this light, direct, and not vague in any way?
7. Exhaust noises and smoke Does the exhaust rattle against the chassis, especially at tickover? Look out for smoke in the mirror, especially when using engine braking to slowing down from a high speed. As noted above: Blue, oil; white, brake fluid; and black, excessive fuel.
8. Speedo and tacho All model have two big gauges that are cable driven. Do the needles waver or wobble, indicating a worn drive cable? Is the calibration of the speedo correct against a sat nav GPS speed reading? (The simplest way to check this is to download a digital speedometer application

Before starting the car from cold, pull the choke out entirely and turn it clockwise a quarter-turn to lock it out. Progressively push it back in (by unlocking and locking, of course) as the engine warms up.

on a smartphone). Safety First: never look at your phone whilst driving. Take a passenger to read the GPS speeds.

9. The four minor gauges

   a. Temperature gauge Does this rise to its mid-point after a couple of miles from a cold start? (Always avoid using heavy acceleration until the engine is quite warm.)

   b. Oil pressure gauge When hot, does it show at least 50psi of pressure at 2000rpm? (Note, it will be higher when cold and lower on hot tickover.)

   c. Fuel gauge Does this read consistently and is it over a quarter full? (This is especially important on the TR5, which often suffer low fuel starvation on left-hand bends.)

   d. Ammeter This sometimes reads a discharge despite all being well, which is due to wiring inconsistencies. To check if charging is working, when stationary, hold the revs at 2000rpm and turn on the headlights. Does the ammeter momentarily show a discharge and then at least return to its previous reading as the charging circuit compensates for the extra load?

10. Comfort Is the seat to your liking? There's no point buying a car that'll leave you needing a chiropractor after every drive. If the roof is on, is it pretty well sealed, especially at speed? It's usual to have a bit of wind noise and the odd draught, but there should be nothing worse than this.

Keep a close eye on the oil pressure. It should read over 50psi at all times (except when a hot engine is ticking over). A lower reading might indicate engine wear.

Paperwork and final considerations

To complete your assessment, consider the following items:

1. Documentation It's vitally important that this is all in order and can be a real deal breaker if it's not. Chapter 11 gives more details of this, but briefly:

   a. Registration document (log book) Do the chassis and engine numbers match the car (see 'under the bonnet' above)? Is the car's description accurate? How many previous owners are listed? (However, a TR in very good

The (optional) overdrive switch is the long stalk on the steering column. It gives an extra (fifth) gear for relaxed high speed running. Don't forget to disengage it as you slow down.

condition with lots of previous owners is still a good buy.) Are the keeper's name and address the same as the person selling it, and the address where you're inspecting it? If not, be very sceptical – if you buy a stolen car, the real owner and their insurers may try to claim it back.

b. Annual safety check documents (MoT) Be aware that all these TRs are more than 40 years old, and consequently, in the UK, it doesn't need an annual safety inspection. If a certificate is present, is it valid? Are there some old ones too, giving a trail of mileage figures to scrutinise?

c. Restoration and other invoices If the owner claims that the TR has had a full restoration, are there invoices present to back this up? Ditto, if it's claimed that the engine has been rebuilt to an unleaded-friendly specification. In general, ignore any claim that isn't backed up with documentation.

d. Main and spare keys Are there keys for the ignition, doors, boot, and glovebox? Do they all work? Are there any spares.

2. Private or trade sale? Although the price will generally be higher with a trade sale, you are protected by the Consumer Rights Act. A trade seller has to give a guarantee that the car is fit for purpose, which can be very useful if things go wrong later.

3. Extra warranty If you buy from a trader, sometimes you'll also be offered a warranty with the car for an additional cost. Beware of these – they are full of beautiful promises, but often they don't pay out as they should. We once recovered a TR that burnt out a piston soon after its purchase from another trader with an extra warranty. Normally, this fault means a full engine rebuild with a new set of matched pistons. However, in this case, the miserly warranty company would only pay for one unmatched piston, no reboring, and minimal labour.

Conclusion
And finally …
- Don't rush into a decision to purchase. Go home and sleep on it.
- Have a private discussion with the friend who hopefully accompanied you, and get their thoughts.
- Don't be pressured into a hasty purchase by promises of a price reduction for a quick sale, or threats that others are also coming to view the same car.

A good purchase will be a joy to own and drive for many years. Take your time to find the right one for you.

Evaluation procedure
Add up the total points:
64 = excellent
48 = good
32 = average
16 = poor

Excellent cars should be close to concours standard, with only a few minor faults. Good cars should be reliable runners, with a small number of faults; hopefully nothing that needs immediate attention, but the assessment should highlight any that do. Average cars will have a number of problems, both minor and major, and will need a careful assessment to inform the potential purchaser of the work required to fix them. Poor cars will potentially require a full restoration.

10 Auctions
– sold! Another way to buy your dream

Auction pros and cons
Pros Auctions operate to trade markets rather than retail, prices are often lower than a dealer and some private sellers. Auctioneers have usually confirmed ownership with the seller, and it should be possible to check this and any other relevant paperwork. You may also receive a 24-hour warranty.

Cons Minimal or vague information before travelling to the venue, and mostly sales-orientated descriptions. To avoid disappointment, learn to read between the lines of the description, and only visit if there are several candidate cars. Star lots may be stored indoors under good light, but there is limited scope to examine cars thoroughly. A wise buyer gets to the venue early and would do well to take this book, a mirror, and a torch. Classic cars cannot be road tested, so for nearby venues, try to arrive early on preview days to see the lots arriving and being offloaded or marshalled into position. The attendants may be prepared to start a car for you. Intended as trade sales, the vehicles often need valeting, which dealers are happy to do; this should not put you off.

Do your research, decide your limit, and stick to it. Remember the auctioneer's charges, or the extra five to ten per cent may come as a shock. Admission is normally by catalogue and usually covers two people, so take a friend; it's amazing what a second pair of eyes can spot.

Catalogue prices and payment details
Auction catalogues and websites usually feature an estimated price and will spell out all charges and acceptable payment methods. Be sure you can comply before bidding. An immediate part-payment or deposit is usually requested if you win, with the balance payable within 24 hours. Check for cash and credit card limits, as well as personal cheque, debit card, or banker's draft options. The car won't be released until all costs are cleared, with storage normally at your expense.

Viewing
It may be possible to view on the day/hours before an auction. Staff or owners may unlock doors, engine, and luggage compartments for inspection, or start the engine. Examining the car is fine, but you can't jack it up, so take a mirror on a stick.

eBay and other online auctions
Online auctions could land you a car at a bargain price, though you'd be foolhardy to bid without examining it first. A useful feature of eBay is that the location of the car is shown, so you can narrow your choices. Be prepared to be outbid in the last few moments of the auction – enter your maximum bid and the site will increase your actual bids in steps as necessary. Your competitors will be doing this, so you must too.

Remember, your bid is binding, and it will be difficult to get restitution in the case of a crooked seller fleecing you – caveat emptor! Let the buyer beware!

Be scam-savvy! Some cars offered for sale online are ghost cars. It's essential that you only pay when you collect the car and have made sure it exists and is as described. Paying by cash or credit (NOT debit) card gives some consumer protection, but never pay by bank transfer before collection, no matter how insistent the seller is about this.

11 Paperwork
– correct documentation is essential!

The paper trail
Classic, collector, and prestige cars usually come with a large portfolio of paperwork accumulated and passed on by a succession of proud owners. This documentation represents the real history of the vehicle, and from it can be deduced the level of care the car has received, how much it's been used, the specialists that have worked on it, what's been spent, and the dates of major repairs and restorations.

All of this information will be priceless to you as the new owner, so be very wary of cars with little paperwork to support their claimed history.

Registration documents
All countries have some form of registration for private vehicles, whether it's like the American 'pink slip' system or the British 'log book' system.

It's essential to check that the registration document is genuine, that it relates to the car in question, and that the vehicle details are correctly recorded, including chassis, VIN, and engine numbers (if shown). If you are buying privately, the seller's name and address will be recorded in the document; this may not be the case if you are buying from a dealer.

In the UK, the vehicle registration certificate (V5C) is printed with detachable coloured sections. The main one states the car's specification, the seller retains a section to send to the DVLA, and you do the same with a third section.

If the car has been off the road for many decades and there is no V5C document, and it has an old green concertina-style log book, you will have to apply for a new V5C to use the car on the road. Be prepared for a lengthy process to try to keep the original registration number, with the possibility that you won't succeed. In this case, the DVLA will issue a new age-related number.

If the car has a foreign registration there will be expensive and time-consuming formalities to complete. Do you really want the hassle?

Roadworthiness certificate
Most country/state administrations require that vehicles are regularly tested to prove they are safe to use on the public highway and do not produce excessive emissions.

In the USA the requirement varies, but most states insist on an emissions test every two years as a minimum, while the police are charged with pulling over unsafe-looking vehicles.

In the UK, after recent changes to the rules, an MoT certificate is not required for all TRs because they are over 40 years old. However, it is still a very good idea to have an annual safety test, as this gives an independent assessment of the car's roadworthiness and provides proof to an insurance company that your car is roadworthy. This could save you a fortune if you are involved in an accident, even if it wasn't your fault, as your insurer will inspect your car and not pay out if it is unsafe.

Old MoT certificates provide a good record of the car's mileage and annual usage. If these are missing, the DVLA government website may be able to fill in the gaps – on the internet, log on to www.gov.uk/check-mot-history. Remember you can submit your car for a MoT test even if there is a current certificate.

Road licence tax

The administration of every country/state charges some kind of tax for the use of its road system. The form of road licence tax, its cost, and how it is displayed, varies enormously around the world.

However, it must be present and valid to drive the car on a public highway legally.

In the UK, all TRs are more than 40 years old and qualify for free road tax. You must still apply in the normal way, but there is no cost. Be aware that changed legislation in the UK means that the current tax is cancelled when a car is sold, and it is the responsibility of the new owner to re-tax the vehicle immediately before driving it. It's therefore vital to receive the car's V5C at the time of purchase so you can obtain the road tax. If the DVLA disputes the age of a car, a car club's records may be able to help you.

In the UK, if a car with a V5C hasn't been used for a period of time, the owner probably has declared it 'off the road' – this is known as SORN (Statutory Off Road Notification). This is automatically cancelled when the tax applied for.

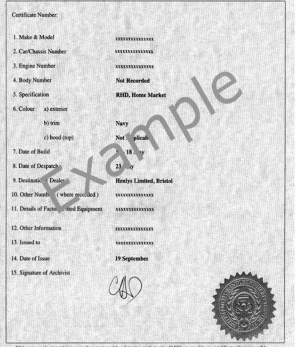

BRITISH MOTOR INDUSTRY HERITAGE TRUST

CERTIFIED COPY OF A FACTORY RECORD

BMIHT certifies that the details given below are a true copy of an entry in the original factory records for the vehicle with the chassis number quoted.

This Certificate does not constitute verification of the present condition of a specific vehicle. These are the details of the car as it left the assembly line. Cars were sometimes modified by the manufacturer after production and prior to shipment.

Certificate Number:

1. Make & Model	xxxxxxxxxxxxxxxx
2. Car/Chassis Number	xxxxxxxxxxxxxxx
3. Engine Number	xxxxxxxxxxxxxx
4. Body Number	Not Recorded
5. Specification	RHD, Home Market
6. Colour a) exterior	
b) trim	Navy
c) hood (top)	Not Applicab
7. Date of Build	18 y
8. Date of Despatch	23 y
9. Destinatic Dealer	Henlys Limited, Bristol
10. Other Numb (where recorded)	xxxxxxxxxxxxxx
11. Details of Facto tted Equipment	xxxxxxxxxxxxxx
12. Other Information	xxxxxxxxxxxxxx
13. Issued to	xxxxxxxxxxxxxx
14. Date of Issue	19 September
15. Signature of Archivist	

While every care has been taken to ensure the correctness of the information supplied neither BMIHT nor any of its associated Trust or Companies will be held liable for any errors or omissions or the consequences thereof. BMIHT accepts no liability if incorrect numbers have been quoted by the enquirer.
BMIHT Registered Office, Banbury Road, Gaydon, Warwick. CV35 0BJ. Registered in England No 1690517. Registered under the Charities Act No 288573.

The British Motor Industry Heritage Trust (BMIHT) will sell you a certificate that records the original build specification and date of your car. See main text for the website address.

Certificates of authenticity

For TR4/4A/5/250, it is possible to get a certificate proving its age and authenticity (eg engine and chassis numbers, paint colour, and trim); Heritage Certificates are very useful, so ask if the car comes with one. If you want to obtain a certificate, go to www.britishmotormuseum.co.uk/archive/heritage-certificates.

If the car has been used in European classic car rallies, it may have a FIVA (Federation Internationale des Vehicules Anciens) certificate.

The so-called 'FIVA Passport,' or 'FIVA Vehicle Identity Card,' enables organisers and participants to recognise if a particular vehicle is suitable for individual events. If you want to obtain such a certificate, go to www.fbhvc.co.uk or www.fiva.org. There will be similar organisations in other countries, too.

Valuation certificate
Hopefully, the seller will have a recent valuation certificate from a recognised expert, stating the value of the particular car. Such documents, together with photos, are usually needed to get 'agreed value' insurance. Generally, such documents should confirm your own assessment of the car's approximate worth; they aren't a guarantee of an exact value, as experts' values never agree precisely. The easiest way to find out how to obtain a formal valuation is to contact one of the specialists listed in chapter 16.

Service history
Try to obtain as much service history and other paperwork about the car as you can. Naturally, dealer stamps, or specialist garage receipts, are the most sought after items. However, everything helps, and items like the original bill of sale, handbook, parts invoices, and repair bills, all add to the story and character of the car. Also, a sales brochure correct to the year of the car's manufacture is well worth having!

Often, these cars will have been serviced at home by their owners with little paperwork to prove it. If this is the case, ask what work was completed, when, and seek some evidence of it being done. Your assessment of the car's overall condition should tell you whether the seller's claims are genuine.

Restoration proof
If the seller claims that the car has been restored, then expect receipts and photographic evidence from a specialist restorer to prove it.

The photos should form a sequence taken while the restoration was under way, and taken at various stages, from multiple angles. This will help you gauge the thoroughness of the work. Before you buy the car, confirm that all the photographs are included in the deal, as they form an important part of the vehicle's history. It's surprising how many sellers are happy to sell their car, but want to hang on to their photographs! In the latter event, you may be able to persuade the vendor to get a set of copies made.

12 What's it worth?
– let your head rule your heart

If you used the marking system in chapter 9, you'll know whether the car is in excellent (maybe concours), good, average, or poor condition. This allows you to assess its value more accurately.

Guide price
You can find a guide to the price of your chosen model in a number of places:

• Classic/collector car magazines often have a price guide in the back.
• An internet search will produce a number of sites that will give you a valuation.
• Classic car auction reports also summarise recent prices realised and are available in print and online.

There will likely be a range of prices offered from these sources, so use all of them to get an idea of a typical price for your chosen TR. Read the condition notes carefully to make sure you are comparing like for like. Also, bear in mind, the most difficult cars to value are concours winning examples with trophies to prove it. If you really want one of these you may have to agree to the seller's higher-than-guide price.

Before you start haggling with the seller, decide what effect on the price the following desirable and undesirable features may have for you.

Desirable features
• Fuel-injection on the six-cylinder cars. Optional improved throttle linkage kit.
• Uprated carburettors on non-PI cars (either larger SU or Weber units).
• Unleaded fuel engine conversion; hardened exhaust valve seats. (Documentary proof needed.)

The ignition distributor (middle) still has the original points (red) and condenser (orange wire) fitted. Electronic ignition gives better power and reliability. Choose either a separate power amplifier system (left) for best performance, or a distributor mounted system (right) for cheapness and an original appearance.

- Spin-on oil filter conversion
- Oil cooler kit. Optional thermostat
- Electric engine fan. Optional manual override
- Alternator conversion on TR4/4A
- Performance exhaust manifold and/or sports stainless exhaust system
- Electronic Ignition conversion
- Bosch fuel pump (on TR5 PI system)
- Alloy rocker cover
- Air horns
- Fifth gear on the gearbox (either an overdrive or an aftermarket five-speed gearbox)
- Galvanised and/or wax injected chassis
- Chassis reinforcements to the front lower suspension mounts and differential mounts (IRS cars only)
- Polyurethane suspension bushes
- Rear telescopic shock absorbers. Optional uprated adjustable shock absorbers.
- Uprated adjustable front shock absorbers
- Uprated front brake pads. optional uprated four-pot callipers and ventilated discs
- Better quality carpets and/or leather seat covers
- Aftermarket seats with improved support (often sourced from Mazda MX5)
- Walnut veneered dashboards (except TR4)
- Auxiliary bonnet release cable
- Anti-theft system(s) (fitted professional alarm, tracker, hidden ignition or PI pump cut-off switch, and/or steering wheel clamp)
- Electric window conversion (provided it works well)
- Sports steering wheel
- Uprated QI headlights and/or LED side/ stop/tail/indicator/ dashboards lights
- Enhanced in-car entertainment system (possibly with a retro appearance)
- Double Duck or Mohair soft top (except Surrey Top cars)
- 12V power socket (for sat navs, etc)
- Improved jack (for spare wheel changing)
- Carpet in the boot
- Surrey top with both steel and fabric roofs
- Lightweight alloy body panels (providing they fit well, and are not fibreglass)

The original TR4/4A thick fanbelt is unreliable and difficult to fit. The thin fanbelt conversion fixes this and also allows a more efficient alternator to be fitted. The 'thick' belt water pump pulley (top arrow) is about to be changed. The alternator has a thin belt pulley (bottom arrow).

- Wider alloy or wire wheels (up to 6Jx15)
- Wider steel radial tyres
- Hardtop option on cars with soft top

Note, original condition enthusiasts will consider many of the above items undesirable!

Undesirable features

- Non-original engine
- TR5 fitted with carburettors
- Non-original paint colour (especially pink or 'cowpat' brown!)
- The engine bay painted a different colour to the rest of the car
- TR4As with a live back axle (25 per cent of American TR4As are made like this; handling is significantly worse than the IRS cars)
- Extremely wide and/or incorrect diameter wheels and tyres. (These alter the gearing, cause speedometer inaccuracy, and can foul the bodywork/suspension)
- Lopsided or crab-tracked suspension (caused by unmatched road springs and badly tracked IRS trailing arm units)
- Excessively low or high ride height (resulting in excessive or inadequate ground clearance)
- Fibreglass body panels
- Extra bonnet bulges and vents (however, works team-styled front wing side vents are acceptable if executed professionally)
- Cheap, cheerful, and poorly-fitting aftermarket bumpers and other chrome items
- Very thin and stretchy vinyl soft tops
- Excessive customisation (extra chrome plating in the engine bay, electric door locks, two-tone paint jobs, button-backed quilted interior trim, non-standard instruments, and hugely flared wheelarches)

Striking a deal

How does the asking price compare with the guide price after factoring in desirable/undesirable features and mileage? Remember to include any dealer or auction premium, too.

Be prepared to negotiate and be realistic about the value – a small compromise on the part of the vendor or buyer will often facilitate a deal at little real cost to either.

The original lever arm rear shock absorbers are too soft. This telescopic conversion on an IRS car cures this problem.

– it'll take longer and cost more than you think

Firstly, we'd better put our cards on the table: we've been professionally restoring TRs for many decades. However, if you're expecting us to extol its virtues for every owner, you could not be more wrong! Restoration is a serious commitment of time and money, and you need to think hard before starting down this road. In fact, at work, prospective customers with new projects in mind are always cautioned to give it serious consideration before starting, as the cost will generally exceed the TR's value when finished.

Why do people restore these cars? There are two main reasons:

To properly restore a chassis, it must be stripped bare, shot-blasted, and mounted on a jig for repair and alignment.

• The car is very special to them, perhaps they or a family member bought it new, so it has to be this car.
• They want to be sure that the vehicle is sound from the chassis upwards, with a full photographic record of the work. Often they will personalise the car during the restoration, adding non-standard paint colour, a tuned engine, tuned suspension, state-of-the-art in-car entertainment system, uprated interior trim, etc. The list is almost endless.

Potential pitfalls to avoid with a professional restoration

So, if you'd think restoration might be for you, make it a success by avoiding these common pitfalls:

1. Don't choose the cheapest estimate; research and choose the most professional well-established firm A while back, an unhappy owner asked us to report on another restorer's work on his recently restored classic car. The restorer's price had been very cheap, and now he had the car back, he understood why! Filler oozed through the unrepaired rust holes inside the wings; the restorer stole his original engine by substituting a similar one from a later model; the trim was the cheapest, most ill-fitting job possible; it drove terribly; and so the list went on. The restorer was

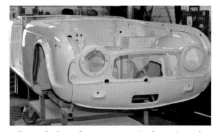

A workshop frame-mounted, restored, and painted TR5 bodyshell is ready to be reattached to the restored chassis.

a sole trader with limited experience, and the owner had just plunged in with no background research on the company. The restorer turned out to be penniless, so there was no chance of a refund, and he had many other unhappy customers too.

2. Visit the restorer often and review the progress of the project The unhappy owner mentioned above never once visited the restorer to see the work in progress, he simply handed over the stage payments. A professional restorer will positively encourage customer visits to review the project and guide the future progress. If they don't do this, beware!

3. Don't start with an incomplete rust bucket Buying such a TR is a cheap initial start to the project, and it may look attractive. However, it's far more expensive in the long run. The many missing parts will be almost impossible to buy because they never wear out, and consequently, no one stocks replacements. If the car has already been stripped down, beware! It probably won't all be there, and what is, probably won't be sorted appropriately. Such a project is like a 10,000 piece jigsaw with the picture on the lid missing! Progress will be very slow and unnecessarily expensive.

4. Don't change horses in midstream! Beware of altering the specification while the project is progressing. If you'd like a concours car, make this very clear right at the beginning; doing so later will likely mean much work will have to be redone at extra cost.

5. Expect the final cost to exceed the estimate Restorations cost what the problems originally inherent in the car cost to fix; many of these will be worse than foreseen. Expect some budget creep, and reserve extra funds to cover this.

6. Don't go for a fixed cost restoration This type of restoration can appear attractive, but stop and think about it for a moment: Is the price so big that the restorer can't lose if the costs creep upwards? If so, you'll be the loser financially.
Is the price so low that the restorer will run out of money and end up cutting corners on the quality? If so, you'll be the loser with a poor quality car.

7. Don't stop a project midway through and expect to get your

The restored rolling chassis is ready to receive the refurbished body shown in the previous picture.

With the body safely back on the rolling chassis, this TR5 is ready for reassembly.

money back by selling it **Part finished projects are always challenging to sell, and the price realised never matches the amount spent to date. If you're not sure you'll have sufficient time or money to finish the work, it's best not to start!**

8. Don't put a fixed timescale requirement on a large project **Don't demand that the car is finished by a specific date, for example, because it's needed for a daughter's wedding or a particular classic car rally. Many factors affect the speed of a project, and often they are out of the control of the restorer. Remember, restoration is a craftsmanship-based industry, not a just-in-time modern production line.**

How you can save money without compromising the quality of the restoration
There are two ways you can do this without incurring heartbreak:

1. Do some or all of the work yourself
   - Do you have sufficient skills and workshop space to tackle all the work yourself? If so, your spare time is free, and lots of money can be saved. Remember, a disassembled car occupies about three times the garage space of an assembled car.
   - If, however, you can only undertake the easier jobs yourself, many professional restorers will be happy to work with you. They do the jobs requiring specialist skills or equipment, and you do the rest. At work, we often restore a TR to a painted rolling bodyshell with the engine and gearbox installed. The owner then reassembles the rest of the car, has fun in the process, and saves a lot of money.

2. Beware of running away with optional extras **These can add a lot to the end cost. At work, if funds for the project are tight, we often advise focussing on the** core essentials first, and deciding on the optional extras (such as enhanced interior trim) later. This way the foundation of the restoration is 100 per cent sound, and you could even leave some of the optional work until later when your funds have recovered.

Part-way through the reassembly process, the TR5 will soon be ready for its trim and roof. You can see the finished car in the introduction chapter of this book.

Conclusion
Use these tips, and you should have a good restoration experience, with a superb TR at the end.

14 Paint problems
– bad complexion, including dimples, pimples and bubbles

Paint faults generally occur due to lack of protection and maintenance, or inadequate preparation before spraying. Some of the following conditions may be present:

Orange peel occurs when the paint is applied too thickly, and subsequent inadequate polishing. It *might* polish out; otherwise, a respray is needed.

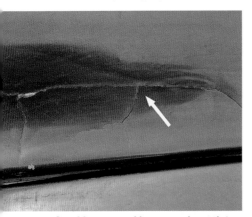

Cracking caused by excessive paint thickness. A bare metal respray is the only remedy.

Orange peel
Appears as an uneven paint surface, similar in look to the skin of an orange – hence the name. The fault is caused by the paint being too thickly applied. Its appearance can sometimes be reduced by using a paint cutting/rubbing compound, or very fine grades of abrasive paper. Consult a bodywork specialist for advice on the particular car.

Cracking
Likely caused by too many layers of paint (usually from numerous resprays), or by an adverse reaction to newly applied paint over old layers. Removing the paint and respraying the problem panel is often the only solution.

Crazing
Similar to cracking, sometimes the paint takes on a crazed appearance, which is caused by a reaction between the underlying surface and the paint. Removing the paint and respraying the problem panel is often the only solution.

Blistering and spider's web veins
It is almost always caused by corrosion of the metal beneath the paint. Usually, a perforation will be found in the metal, and the damage will be worse than is suggested by the area of blistering. The metal will have to be repaired before repainting.

Micro blistering
Usually the result of a cheap respray, when moisture is trapped beneath the top coats. It can also be caused by car covers that don't breathe and cause the paint

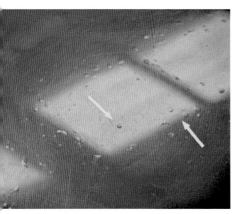

Micro blisters appear when the primer layers beneath are contaminated. A bare metal respray is the only antidote.

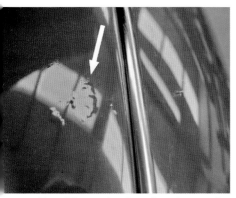

Rust blisters develop when the panel rusts. Panel repair or renewal, followed by a bare metal respray, is the only cure.

to sweat. Paint removal and respraying the problem area is normally the only solution.

Fading
Some colours, especially reds, are prone to fading if subjected to intense sunlight for extended periods, even with the benefit of polish protection. Sometimes, proprietary paint restorers and/or paint cutting/rubbing compounds will retrieve the situation. However, a respray is often the only real solution.

Peeling
Often a problem with metallic paintwork, and occurs when the sealing lacquer topcoat becomes damaged and begins to peel off. Poorly applied paint may also peel. The remedy is to strip and start again!

Dimples and fish eyes
Caused by polish residue (particularly silicone types) not being properly removed before respraying, causing the paint to be repelled as it dries. Paint removal and repainting is the only solution.

Dents
Small dents are often easily cured by Paintless Dent Removal (PDR) specialists such as www.dentmasteruk.co.uk. They suck or push out the dent (as long as the paint surface is still intact). Companies offering dent removal services usually come to your home; search the internet for a local expert.

Colour mismatch
Sometimes various panels will be a slightly different colour to the rest of the car. Caused by the panels being sprayed at different times and from different batches of paint. The only cure is a full respray.

15 Problems due to lack of use
– just like their owners, TRs need exercise!

Cars, like humans, experience problems if regular exercise is neglected.

How to minimise these problems

1. A weekly run of at least ten miles is recommended for classic cars if conditions are dry, the car is taxed, it's insured, and roadworthy. If these circumstances don't apply, run the car with the back wheels jacked up and axle stands under the chassis until everything is nicely warm. Go up and down through the gears. Always think safety – properly chock the front wheels and choose a well-ventilated area.
3. Leave the handbrake off, so the rear brake drums don't seize up. Instead, chock the wheels and leave it in a low gear.
4. Keep the antifreeze to the correct level. Your car's components can still freeze when inside your garage during the winter months.
5. Change the oil and filter regularly. Engine oil gets increasingly corrosive with age, even when it is parked up.
6. Leave the soft top up. If fitted, you must store this in its raised position. A folded soft top will shrink, while the back window will get cloudy and creased in storage, especially if it's wet. The extra effort to raise the soft top after each journey is well worth it.

To run a laid-up or unroadworthy TR, jack the back wheels off the ground, apply axle stands and front wheel chocks, and then run the car up and down through the gears to get the engine and transmission thoroughly warm.

Problems through lack of use

When looking at a potential purchase that has had limited use, its condition will depend on the storage environment and time it has been stored as well as any pre-storage preparations. Bear in mind that the following problems are likely to be experienced:

Unused brakes go rusty. Light surface rust like this will clean up in use. Deep-seated rust may require disc renewal.

- Engine pistons are prone to seizing in its bores. If so, try putting the car in top gear and manually rocking it back and forwards until you see the crankshaft pulley move. If this fails, remove the sparkplugs and put a little diesel or paraffin into each sparkplug hole, leave it for a week or so, and try again. If successful, change the oil to remove the contamination, and run the engine as soon as possible.
- Hydraulic brake cylinders can seize, and you'll find that when you push the brake pedal, the wheels lock solid and stay that way. If so, jack the car and free up each wheel in turn.
- Often due to surface rust, the clutch plate can stick to the flywheel and prevent the gears from engaging. The correct remedy is to remove the gearbox and change the clutch. You could also try turning the engine on the starter with the clutch pedal fully depressed, fourth gear selected, the handbrake on, and the wheels well chocked. Be prepared for the car to jerk forward.
- Rubber hoses perish, crack, and leak. This is especially true of older rubber fuel hoses when used with modern petrol.
- Metal cables and pipes can seize up.
- The battery goes flat and refuses to take a charge. If so, it must be renewed. If the terminals fur up, hot water from a kettle washes this away, and petroleum jelly on the terminals stops it reforming.
- Shock absorbers can seize, leak, or creak and groan. If so, renewal is needed.
- Tyres will perish when old and show cracking, especially on the sidewalls. If parked in the same place for a long time, a tyre will gain a semi-permanent flat spot, and will become impossible to balance for a smooth ride.
- The exhaust system can rust through, leak, and get noisy. If so, renewal is usually needed.
- Fuel goes stale over time, turning dark yellow and smelling awful! If so, starting will be difficult. Drain the petrol tank and refill with fresh fuel.

16 The Community
– key people, organisations and companies in the TR world

Clubs
The Triumph TR6 and 250 Club of America (6-PACK) PO Box 30064, Cincinnati, OH 45230, USA. E-mail: membership@6-pack.org www.6-pack.org.

TR Drivers Club 17 Burgundy Close, Locksheath, Southampton, Hants, SO81 6PS, England. Tel: 01562 825000. trdriver@btinternet.com.

TR Register 1B Hawksworth, Southmead Industrial Park, Didcot, Oxon, OX11 7HR, England. Tel: 01235 818866. tr.register@onyxnet.co.uk, www.tr-register.co.uk.

Vintage Triumph Register 15218 West Warren Avenue, Dearborn, MI 48126, USA. vtr-www@www.vtr.org, www.vtr.org.

UK main spares suppliers
Moss-Europe Hampton Farm Estate, Hanworth, Middlesex, TW13 6DB, England. Tel: 020 8867 2020. sales@moss-europe.co.uk.

Revington TR Home Farm, Middlezoy, Somerset, TA7 0PD, England. Tel: 01823 698 437. info@revingtontr.com www.revingtontr.com.

Rimmer Bros Sleaford Road, Bracebridge Heath, Lincoln, LN4 2NA England. Tel: 01522 568 000. sales@rimmerbros.co.uk.

TR Bitz Lyncastle Way, Barley Castle Trading Estate, Appleton Thorn, Warrington, Cheshire, WA4 4ST England. Tel: 01925 861 861. triumph@trbitz.u-net.com.

TR Enterprises Dale Lane, Blidworth, Mansfield, Nottinghamshire, NG21 0SA England. Tel: 01623 793 807. stevehall@trenterprises.com.

TRGB Ltd Unit 1 Sycamore Farm Industrial Estate, Long Drove, Somersham, Huntingdon, Cambs, PE17 3HJ, England. Tel: 01487 842 168. www.trgb.co.uk.

Friendly TR owners like to get together, especially when members of a club. Search online for clubs and meets in your neighbourhood.

US main spares suppliers

The Roadster Factory PO Box 332, Killen Road, Armagh, PA 15920, USA. Tel: (800) 678-8764. www.the-roadster-factory.com.

Moss Motors PO Box 847, 440 Rutherford Street, Goleta, CA 93116, USA. Tel: (800) 667-7872. www.mossmotors.com.

Victoria British Ltd Box 14991, Lenexa, KS 66285-4991, USA. Tel: (800) 255-0088. www.longmotor.com.

Overdrive repair specialists

Overdrive Repair Services Units C3/4 Ellisons Road, Norwood Industrial Estate, Killamarsh, Sheffield, S21 2JG England. Tel: 0114 248 2632. www.overdrive-repairs.co.uk/products.

Overdrive spares Unit A2 Wolston Business Park, Main Street, Wolston, Nr Coventry, CV8 3FU. England. Tel: 02476 543 686. odspares@aol.com.

Chassis remanufacture

CTM Engineering Unit 3A, Bury Farm, Curbridge, Nr Botley, Hants SO30 2HB, England. Tel: 01489 782054. colin@ctmeng.freeserve.co.uk.

Books

Triumph TR6 by William Kimberley. Veloce.
How to Restore Triumph TR5/250 &TR6 by Roger Williams. Veloce.
How to Restore Triumph TR2/3/3A/4/4A by Roger Williams. Veloce.
How to Improve Triumph TR5, 250 & 6 by Roger Williams. Veloce.
Original Triumph TR: The Restorers Guide to TR2/3/3A/4/4A/5/250/6 by Bill Piggott.
Triumph TR2/3/3A/4/4A Workshop Manual. Haynes.
Triumph TR5 & TR6 Workshop Manual. Haynes.
Triumph TR4 & TR4A Workshop Manual (official publication). Brooklands Books.
Triumph TR5 PI Workshop Manual Supplement (official publication). Brooklands Books.
Triumph TR - TR2 to 6: The last of the traditional sports cars by Bill Piggott. Veloce.

Parts catalogues (very useful and usually free of charge)

TR2-4A Parts Catalogue and *TR5-6 Parts Catalogue* by Moss. sales@moss-europe.co.uk, www.mossmotors.com.
TR2-5 Parts Catalogue by Rimmer Bros. sales@rimmerbros.co.uk.

Other specialist suppliers, books and catalogues

Search the Internet for the most up-to-date information!

Other useful organisations

HPI finance check	www.hpicheck.com
DVLA – MOT History	www.check-mot.service.gov.uk
DVLA – MOT & Tax Status	www.gov.uk/check-vehicle-tax
AA	www.theaacarcheck.com
RAC	www.rac.co.uk/buying-a-car/rac-car-data-check

17 Vital statistics
– essential data at your fingertips

TR4

Engine Water-cooled 2138cc/130in^3 four-cylinder OHV. Iron block and head with wet liners. Twin SU or Stromberg carburettors. 100bhp in standard tuning.
Gearbox Four-speed manual with optional overdrive on 2nd, 3rd, and 4th gears.
Brakes Single-circuit operating front discs and rear drums. No servo.
Suspension (F) Dual wishbones and telescopic shock absorbers.
Suspension (R) Live rear axle and semi-elliptic leaf springs.
Tyres 165R15, 4.5J15 wheels
Performance 0-60mph: 10.7sec, top speed: 110mph
Average fuel consumption 25mpg
Unladen weight 2240lb/1016kg
Dimensions Length: 3902mm (154in). Width: 1470mm (58in). Height: 1170mm (46in). Wheelbase: 2240mm (88in).
Chassis numbers CTxxxxx-LO (L, left-hand drive; O, overdrive)
(Chassis plate is on the rear scuttle panel under the bonnet)
Approximate production dates 1961, CT1-CT2470; 1962, CT2471-CT18403; 1963, CT18404-CT28485; 1964, CT28486-CT40000; 1965, CT40001-CT40304
Engine numbers CTxxxxx. The digits are a different number from the chassis number. Engine plate is on left hand side of the block by the ignition coil.

TR4A

As for the TR4 except:

Engine 104bhp
Unladen weight 2218lb/1007kg
Suspension (R) IRS Semi-trailing arms, driveshafts, and lever arm shock absorbers.
Average fuel consumption 26mpg
Chassis numbers CTCxxxxx-LO (Chassis plate is on the rear scuttle panel under the bonnet)
Approximate production dates 1965, CTC50001-CTC63736; 1966, CTC63737-CTC75000; 1967, CTC75001-CTC78684 (July '67)
(Note, Live axle TR4As have chassis number CT50001 onwards)
Engine number CTCxxxxx. The digits are a slightly different number from the chassis number. Engine plate is on left hand side of the block by the ignition coil.

TR5 PI

Engine Water-cooled 2498cc/152in^3 fuel-injected straight six-cylinder straight OHV. Iron block and head.150bhp in standard tuning.
Gearbox four-speed manual with optional overdrive on 2nd, 3rd, and 4th gears.
Brakes Dual-circuit close-coupled servo operating front discs and rear drums.
Suspension (F) Dual wishbones and telescopic shock absorbers.
Suspension (R) IRS: Semi trailing arms, driveshafts, and lever arm shock absorbers.
Tyres 165R15, 4.5J15 wheels
Performance 0-60mph: 8.8sec, top speed: 120mph
Average fuel consumption 20mpg

Unladen weight 2268lb/1030kg
Dimensions **Length:** 3902mm (154in). Width: 1470mm (58in). Height: 1170mm (46in). Wheelbase: 2240mm (88in)
Chassis numbers CPxxxx-LO
(Chassis plate is on the left-hand wheelarch under the bonnet)
Approximate production dates 1967, CP1 (Aug '67)-CP585;
1968, CP586-CP3101 (Sept '68)
Engine numbers CPxxxx. The digits are a slightly different number from the chassis number. Engine number is stamped on a lip on left hand side of the block by number five sparkplug.

TR250
As for the TR5 except:

Engine Twin Stromberg carburettors. 111bhp in standard trim.
Performance 0-60mph 10.6s, top speed 109mph
Average fuel consumption 27mpg
Chassis numbers CDxxxx-LO
(Chassis plate is on the left hand wheelarch under the bonnet)
Approximate production dates 1967, CD1 (July '67)-CD2684;
1968, CD2685-CD8594 (Sept '68)
Engine numbers CCxxxx. The digits are a slightly different number from the chassis number. Engine number is stamped on a lip on left hand side of the block by number five sparkplug.

Factory colour codes

TR4/4A		TR5/250	
Paint	Trim	Paint	Trim
Black 11	Black 11	Black 11	Black 11
New White 19 (Early cars – Spa White)	Matador Red 12	New White 19	Matador Red 12
Triumph Racing Green 25	Light Tan 13 (TR4A only)	Triumph Racing Green 25	Light Tan 13
Wedgwood Blue 26 (Early cars – Powder Blue)	Midnight Blue 16	Wedgwood Blue 26	Midnight Blue 16
Signal Red 32		Signal Red 32	Shadow Blue 27
Royal Blue 56 (TR4A only)		Jasmine Yellow 34	
Valencia Blue 66 (TR4A only)		Royal Blue 56	
British Racing Green 75		Valencia Blue 66	
Conifer Green 125		Conifer Green 125	

The Essential Buyer's Guide™ series ...

Index